T0157567

Emotions ...
Justified
Writings

❖

ETREC J. WHITE

iUniverse, Inc.
Bloomington

Emotions ... Justified Writings

iUniverse books may be ordered through booksellers or by contacting:

iUniverse
1663 Liberty Drive
Bloomington, IN 47403
www.iuniverse.com
1-800-Authors (1-800-288-4677)

ISBN: 978-1-4697-9570-6 (sc)
ISBN: 978-1-4697-9569-0 (hc)
ISBN: 978-1-4697-9568-3 (e)

Library of Congress Control Number: 2012904489

Printed in the United States of America

iUniverse rev. date: 3/1/2012

To the most beautiful person in the world to me, and that is my daughter, Elysha White. I haven't always said the right thing or been there for you the way you wanted or needed me to be, but I love you so much, princess, and through it all, we have maintained a bond that nobody can break! Everything that I do in this world is solely about you; I never want to tarnish anything that we have built together, so I hold what we have on the highest pedestal! I love you, Lee-Lee!

~ Daddy ~

Aunt Linda, words can't express all that you've meant and mean to me! I love you so much; I have learned so much from you. You are truly a woman of God! You have always told me to walk by faith and not by sight. I still live up to the words; even when I know that I'm not right, you have instilled so much into me. I just want to say thank you for everything, from our talks to your prayers for me, but, most of all, for your unconditional love!

~ Your Nephew ~

Acknowledgments

I thank God for giving me the ability to express myself in the form of writing the way I do. I give you all the praise! I know that you will make all my dreams come true!

To my family who is my inspiration for everything I do. Knowing that we all have one another gives me the strength to work hard and never to lose focus, even when you all don't see it. My mother, Melba Dale; Dorthea White; and my dad, Hayward White—I love you all so much. The Harris family and the Greene family, I love you all; my aunts, uncles, and cousins. Wilbur Holland Harris (Poppa), I love you; Barbera Greene (Me-Me), I love you!

To my brothers—Elliot White, Christopher Dale, and Richard Scott—I'm nothing without you three! I love you boys to death!

To my other family, all the people who have a special place in my heart for many different reasons: Bishop Edward Robinson and all of the Southside C.O.G.I.C family; Kisha Brown; Tricia Brown; Tychell Clark; Antonio Curry; Chrys Herring; David Jackson; Christopher Andrews (my big bruh); Riley Thomas; Corey Davis; my godmother Elaine Jones; my lil sis Nikki Jones; Tameka Taylor; Stephen Davis; Alesha Gray; Lisa Dogan; Veronica Bolton; Latoya Joyner; Aleshia Chisolm; Jarvis Johnson; Shalisa Wildridge and family; William Wilkins; John Marshall; Chris Macdonald; That PINE FOREST Crew; Dion Viera; Stephanie Wilson; Keysha Webster and family; Johnathan (Neko) Lundy; Christopher (Blackie) Davis; Elizabeth and Robert Edwards; Joseph Mims; Andre and Rita Austin (Maiysha, Keena, Renita, and Aundrea); Ms. Paulette Walker; Robert Spurlock; Marc Lucce; Ms. Gilda Opher (my other momma! I love you still!); Chalkey Haden; my best friends in the whole wide world, Jovan Lewis, and Tomika Rodall; Sidney Fowler; Xavier Hicks; Kimberly Hardy; Nakia Hooks; Randy Thomas; Gregory Campbell; Anthony and Jennifer Shealer (I love you two! I'm forever in your debt!); my football teammates, (Anthony Hamlett; C.J. Hamlett; Reggie Whisenton; Terrance Saturday; John Payne; Torrance Middlebrooks; Tony Stroud; Lendale Bell; Kareem Goodwin; Nathan Murphy; Ronnie White; Tony Bello; William

Fields; Eric Hinton); my publisher, iUniverse, for allowing me to display my talents; and my photographer, Ms. Cynthia for bringing out the best in me!

Special, special thanks to my readers. You could have selected any book, but you chose me and I am grateful to you for your support. If you are that one person I speak to through these pages, my job is complete!

LOVE: Phases of Love

CREATIVITY: Plagues My Mind

EMOTIONS: These Thoughts, These Feeling

SEXUAL HEALING: Erotic Pleasures

"Though we are miles away,
I love you so much, and I'm glad you are my child."

Interlude for Elysha

LOVE:
Phases of Love

What Is Love?

What is love if there isn't any feeling in it?
You can't fake it, front on it, or even pretend with it.
It's not just an emotion, and it doesn't start with looks;
it stems from within, even when you're nervous or shook by
what your significant other is thinking or
what she experiences.

What is love if there isn't any commitment?
You can be together and still not have companionship.
Love isn't just some feeling that comes and goes;
it's something you build on, to season it, water it,
and watch it grow!

What is love if there isn't any friendship in it?
A unity, a bond, more like a forevership! With
love comes trust, with trust comes us, totally
committed, 'cause what is love if I don't have
you in it?

Love Is Deep

My love is deep …
no need to look further …
it's all about us,
so that makes our love unique!
We go through things in life,
that makes us wonder …
no matter what we go through,
good or bad …
we can make it
'cause our love is stronger!
Our love is solid and concrete!
I was only halfway, more like 180 …
till I made things straight with you,
a full 360, to make my life complete!
We get the sideways looks …
'cause we are together.
We are complete opposites,
but that's even better!
Opposites attract!
And though we are different,
there's nothing wrong with that!
I get the best of you,
like you get the best of me …
I love you forever,
I'm in it for the long haul …
I want us stable with longevity!
So despite the mistakes we made,
and those that are yet to come …
I will always be by your side,
and never run!
I love you for you,
despite what people see …
it's all about us,
'cause for you …
my love is deep!

Love with You

I pouted …
thought about it,
hit the pavement,
while I fretted.
Truth of the matter,
I haven't fallen out of love
with you yet.
I tried and tried
to get you out of my heart
and get you out of my mind.
I tried to hate you
just to get you out of my thoughts,
but the more I did …
I felt your presence coming across!
I told myself
that my feelings for you had died,
but truthfully speaking …
to myself …
I lied!
Up late at night,
yeah, I even cried …
thinking about how much I love you,
and why!
The love was never the problem,
it was just some of my actions …
you wanted to elevate things,
instead of simple satisfactions …
I want that to happen,
but I know things might be too late.
You ask me to be honest,
but that is why I hesitate.
I know you don't feel the way I do …
so I'll keep my thoughts to myself,
because you already know that I
haven't fallen out of love with you!

Love Song

When I look at you, I think to myself, *My, my, my,*
'cause I'm so glad that you're my sweet lady,
and ever since I saw those pretty brown eyes,
I knew that you were one in a million.
So, I want you to be forever my lady.
You've April-showered me with your love
and though it's been tough and it seems
like we've been to the end of the road,
it's times like this when every little step I take
makes me love everything about you!

It's times when it is infatuation when I think,
How am I so lucky to have someone like you in
my life?
Though you're a freak like me, you so classy
and jazzy, and a real woman in the streets!
I think about you, and at times I miss you,
so I know that as soon as I see you, I
cancel my plans for a meeting in the bedroom!
So, please excuse my hands, 'cause tonight
they are going to be all over your body, and
I hope you lose control,
'cause between the sheets as I look at you
I know that you are where I want to be!

Baby, you're my tender love, and with everything
that goes on, I know that we can stand the rain,
so I promise that, no matter what we go through,
I will always and forever stay by your side,
and eventually let's get married so forever we can
celebrate our anniversary.

When You're in Love

When you're in love, true love, you will know,
because of how you will feel, because your
life will seem just like a dream
that's turning real.

You will find you're happy any time and at
any place, if you can see a certain
smile upon a certain face.

Because the bright tomorrows that you're looking
forward to will seem to need someone there
to share them all with you.

When you're in love, true love, forever love,
you will surely know, because each day,
the whole day through, your heart will tell
you so!

Because of you, all of my dreams have
come true. The moments we share are
special because of love …
the love we share is special,
because of you!

Crush

I long for your touch.
When I'm near you,
it's an adrenaline rush.
I'm constantly looking at you,
'cause I can't get enough
of your smile,
especially that sexy persona
that makes me blush!
I guess you know
this is more than a crush!

Our connection, for whatever reason,
brought us back together,
but
a lot of time has passed us by,
but it's still whatever!
You have been through your situations,
I have been through mine—
as long as we communicate and remain open,
everything else will be fine.
I'm just coming at you for real.
I usually don't speak my feelings,
but this is how you make me feel.
You have me stepping out of my element.
I've been longing for you for a while;
I guess you're heaven sent!
Ever since
We started talking,
I guess it was evident
that, being around you,
I loved your presence.

Daydreaming

Daydreaming about what I've been longing for, I've been knowing you, but at the same time, I've always prayed for someone like you. You are a blessing, so don't walk away, because it's too early for me to lose you!

We haven't had time to take a walk in a field of flowers, or watch the sunset in the weary sky, or lay on the beach and let the tide beat against the rocks as we kiss, or let our hearts sink when we say good-bye.

In my dreams I see us holding hands, gazing into each other's eyes, when silence will fall because our eyes will be dancing. *I love you,* we both will reply. When I hear your quiet voice and your soft hands caress my face, my stomach turns out of nervousness, and I dream of another place ...

a place where the clouds hang low, where the music is like a peaceful silhouette, and we will be singing the harmony, and I will thank the Lord, because for you, I am in his debt.

My Promise of Love to You

I promise to give you the best of myself and to ask of you
no more than you can give.

I promise to accept you the way you are. I fell in
love with you for the qualities and outlook on life that
you have, and I won't try to shape you into a
different image.

I promise to respect you as a person with you own interests,
desires, and needs, and to realize that those are sometimes
different, but no less important, than my own.

I promise to share with you my time and my close attention, and to
bring joy, strength, and imagination to our relationship.

I promise to keep myself open to you, to let you see through
the window of my personal world into my innermost fears,
feelings, secrets, and my dreams.

I promise to grow along with you, to be willing to face change
as we both change in order to keep our relationship alive
and exciting.

I promise to love you in good times and in bad, with
all I have to give and all I feel inside, in the only way
I know how …
completely and forever.

Worth the Wait

I can't even explain how I feel …
It's like a dream that's become
all so real …
Before you, it was the typical drill,
broads getting on my nerves, make-ups
to break up till I would finally peel.
Asking me to open up, so my heart I would spill,
but it got ripped out and broken
to where I was ready to kill!

But that's not me, because I've changed my ways
to put all the dead drama to the side
so I can enjoy better days!
We've both had our issues and pain we
had to escape,
and though we prolonged our status,
you were worth the wait!

So for you, I'll go that extra mile,
because you the reason my heart
can finally smile!

Plain and Clear

It didn't make sense to me.
I don't know what it is that is affecting me!
Now I clearly see that I have been in love with you since elementary!
You have my emotions going crazy;
emotionally
my head is messed up;
mentally
my heart is pounding through my chest when I'm near you;
physically
I know you can help me get to where I need to be;
spiritually
I know that I messed up, but I know you should be with me,
'cause I'm always thinking about you, and I know that you're constantly
thinking of me!
Let's stop all the playing of games, 'cause with us together, we can do some
serious things equally!
Make my one plus your one and equal our unity!

Untitled 1

We started off as friends, but whoever thought that
we would get to this point? More than just distant lovers
who share a common interest in each other's lives, we
both have steered left and right when we should have kept
straight, but during the crossroads faith brought us back
together again. And I love you deeply 'cause we are more
than just friends, we can talk about whatever at any given
time and clear our thoughts to be just fine.

There are times when our attitudes play a distinctive part,
but that's just something we have to work on without tearing
us apart. I'm glad that I have you in my corner, 'cause there are
times when I need you to lean on, and you can count on me to be
there when you aren't feeling strong.

I often say forget what everybody thinks or says, 'cause this is
something that we have to do on our own. I know that they have
they input, which is cool, but it ain't condoned! I know, whatever I need,
that I can count on you;, and times when you need me, I will be there
for you, so with this in mind, remember that though we go through
our lil situations, I still love you to death and I'm glad you are back in my
life.

It's like this:

It's like this: Sexually, you make me comfortable, to where I can give you my all and do what feels good and not feel ashamed.

Mentally, you keep me focused and assure me things eventually work out for the better and not to stress every detail.

Emotionally, you show me that giving my heart is okay and to break away from the past and focus on us and the now.

Spiritually, you accept me and my faults and push me to continue seeking guidance and prayer for us both!

Nothing can bring me down, 'cause all of this is because of you! You keep me grounded and uplifted,

keeping me inspired:

Keep writing, because you're so gifted!

you keep telling me!

And one day, people are going to see you the way I see you

you keep telling me!

It's like this: You make me feel like nobody has ever made me feel before, and though we are at this point, I know that it's so much more, I want so much more

not only for me, but for us,

so let's elevate our maybe to definite trust!

It's like this: You believe in me like I believe in you, and whatever we go through, it's always going to be about me and you!

Have faith in me, 'cause it's like this: These four attributes are how I adore you —

sexually, mentally, emotionally, and spiritually!

Blessing in Disguise

Who knew? Nobody—hell, not even me or you—
that you would be the one that I opened up to!
Since it's been you, I feel like I'm at a whole other place
that I haven't felt in a while, and it's a feeling that can't be replaced!
Your beautiful smile keeps me getting through my day
even when the clouds block the sun and turn blue skies gray!
I'm funny, but you silly and it's wild to me
that when we do have an intellectual and intelligent conversation,
we are on the same level, and that's unique to me!
We've kind of had the same similarities when it comes to being with others,
passing up on the ones that we should and making the wrong ones lovers.
Hopefully you sense that I'm different from the rest.
I just want you for you; I want your heart to cherish and caress!
See, I wanna be the one to surprise you for lunch,
or on a Saturday morning, feed you your Cinnamon Toast Crunch!
I wanna be the one you can lean on and turn to,
that no matter what, I got your back in all that you go through.

Naturally, there are going to be those moments when we just
get on each other's last nerve!
But just because times are hard, me opting out
would be simply absurd!
So I take you for you, good, bad, and indifferent, realizing that
we are two different people and we might not always see eye to eye.
That's cool with me, 'cause we can take on any obstacle
to make things complete!
I can't wait to see those happy tears in your eyes,
'cause who knew? Nobody—hell, not even me or you—
that you were my blessing in disguise!

Over Again

That perfume is wearing you,
instead of you wearing that perfume,
that elegant dress is amazing,
and you're more than just beautiful!
My heart just skipped two beats,
from the way you batted
tour beautiful eyes.
Though we are loving to one another,
I still have a surprise—
well, it's more of a request.
I thought you were the best,
at figuring me out so
I decided to do something different
and take another route.
See, I had you put on
your elegant dress for more
than a specific reason,
though you are so sexy,
and eye appealing
I chose tonight to fall in love
with you again.
So the thief I will play
'cause your heart I'm stealing!
In the backseat
is a note that you should read;
there is a series of notes,
Like a scavenger hunt; follow each note,
so you will get to your main surprise.
If you're ready, then proceed.
I'm just sitting back
watching you tear up the house.
You want to ask me for clues,
but you know I'm not
going to open up my mouth!
After a couple of hours, finally,
you have reached the clue, and
you hand me the note
with this look on your face
asking what you should do.

Sit down, because the final surprise
is easy—it's me!
Thank you for loving me
and accepting me.
You are more than my other half,
you're more than my best friend.
It's just things like this
that makes me fall in love
with you all over again.

Two Words

Part I

Inviting eyes …
beautiful smells …
Lovely complexion …
smooth skin …
mesmerizing smile …
I see
on you!

God fearing …
God blessed …
your body …
uhhh … yes …
sweet attitude …
soulful heart …
loves kids …
that's a
beautiful thing …

That's why
I feel
you're my
best friend
and my
girlfriend.
I think—
hell, naw,
I do—
love you.
Do you …
love me?
Thank you.

This is
too easy.
To my …
future wife …
will you …

can you ...
marry me?
Please, boo?

So for
you to
always see
that way
when you
think of
two words
you will
always think of

the day
that I
proposed to
my love,
my heart,
my everything.

Love Committed

Here's to you—
more like, here is to us,
a lifetime of commitment,
love, and trust.
To say I love you
is a mere understatement;
I thank God every day
For our love level's placement!
I will honor your thoughts,
treat them as my own,
be an example of love
so people can see us in that form.
All days won't be good, but
all days won't be bad …
when we think of how strong our bond is,
we will sit back and laugh
at all of the petty things
that got us upset,
and we'll reminisce as if this
was a test.
Our love will never fade,
and our love will never die!
It will be used as a tool, so
Others can copy it and comply.
I love you today, tomorrow, and
Forever, always …
when the sky is blue
or things are dismal and gray.
I know no other love but yours
and I know that this is what true lovers dream of!

Modern-Day Love

See, our love is something that we can't forget.
It's unique, and edgy,
trendy,
something others can't detect.
Though we are alike,
actually we're quite different,
from two different sides,
like Montagues and Capulets.
So, I'll say I'm Romeo,
while you're my Juliet.
Envision us, like they were
in the past.
Us, being together?
That's impossible …
Some look crazy,
some make gestures,
others laugh.
Like servants to Juliet;
Your friends are haters,
with the *y'all would never last!*
My friends are like Romeo's cousins,
loud, obnoxious,
tipsy and buzzin',
ready for things to pop off, so
they can shake something!
But I'm not really the tough guy,
and in all actuality, I'm laid back,
down to earth and a lil shy.
You already had the wrong impression;
you thought I was a flashy guy
and that I was just a pretty boy,
and with my looks, that I was just
getting by,
that I dressed real nice, and
that I stay fly!
That's really not me, as you can see!
It wasn't that I was acting funny;
it's just that I'm scared of letting
people get close to me.

See, in a sense we are like
Romeo and Juliet, going through
trials and tribulations,
opening our hearts to love,
and life's situations.
We keep things moving,
we keeping things pushing,
we do things while others
keep looking,
continuing to keep things thriving,
each other's backbone,
conquering dreams and still striving.
I love my Juliet, and I promise
I will not let anyone interfere.
You will always have my heart,
whether far away or near.
So our love I pray
will always continue to grow,
'cause I will love you forever!
Signed, your real-life Romeo.

Reminder to My Wife

I never knew that this moment
would come in my life.
It all feels so right
'cause you across from me,
and I'm thinking, *this is my wife!*
See, you changed my ways …
you changed my life …
I'm more focused on goals
and doing what's right.
Hard times will come,
but with you,
everything will be all right!

Now you're walking down the aisle,
and I see the tears of joy.
I can't help but smile …
See, we have taken our love
to another level
'cause it's unique;
and all too special.
It's kind of a surreal feeling,
but the more I look at you,
I already know the reason.

It wasn't a season,
or the sun and moon
aligned right,
it was you being you
that made me ask you
to be my wife,
so this day is ours,
mine and yours,
together forever,
with honesty and trust.
There's nothing in this world
I wouldn't do for you
'cause you're my baby forever,
and forever I will love you!

Just Because You Are You

My worries are gone, my mind is at ease,
'cause when I think of you, I feel so much peace.
You make me laugh and smile and make me feel complete,
and I haven't felt that in a while.
Soothing, yet calm, is your voice's delight,
to make wrong feel all so right!
We've both had our ups and downs, smiles and frowns,
roads of upcoming, instead of hellward bound.
You allow me to be me, whether that's good or bad,
whether I'm clowning or quiet, happy or sad.
It's a lovely feeling to share yourself with someone;
it's even better when the two become one.
There's plenty of time to get to that level, so for now
I'll look at you as someone real special.

Someone who is down and views the world like I do,
someone I can unite with and pour my heart into.
I'm realistic, so I know every day won't be good; there will be times
when we dislike each other, whether we agree or misunderstand.
But I will respect you and view your thoughts as my own,
put you on the highest pedestal, give you your own throne.
That time will come when we can unite, you and I,
from Me to Us, so for now we'll still do what
we have been doing—keeping cool and being patient.

So I render my thoughts to you, 'cause this is just
how I feel, 'cause since we've been talking, it's been nothing
but real. I can't close this with a hug; I can't close this with a kiss,
so I'll be a lil creative and do something like this: Close your eyes
and picture us wherever, and when you open them … smile … and
read this letter!

At the Spur of the Moment

At the spur of the moment as I get up,
I think about you and how I can't get enough
of your love, your smiles, your look, and your touch!
It's funny, 'cause I love you so much!
I'll admit that we go through our bullshit
and ups and downs, our tears, our joy,
the smiles and frowns.

I pray for us regularly, so I know that when
praises go up, blessings come down!
Its wild, 'cause we in two different towns,
but the presence you have, I swear, I feel you around!
I wish I could change so many things that we have gone through,
then I think back and say naw, 'cause I would never have met you!

Sometimes I get misty eyed and real sentimental
'cause I love everything about you, from physical to mental!
Its times when I'm alone that it hurts me so bad,
to hear you voice on the phone,
and its only 'cause I can't have you in my arms
when everything is bad and when my days go wrong.

At the spur of the moment, my thoughts are clear;
I guess I'm being selfish 'cause I really want you here.
I love your mind, your thoughts, your walk and your talk.
I love the way you make love to me, and the way you break me off.
I love your lips, your eyes, your tongue, and your thighs.
I love when I'm in the middle of you and you give me that white surprise!

You're so classy and jazzy in the street,
but my freak in the bed. I love everything you do,
from the 69 to your head!
I love everything about you, and I want you to know this.
I know things are hard, but I love and adore this relationship!

Though we bump heads and don't agree, I don't condone it,
but I had to write you this when I woke up 'cause this is how I felt
at the spur of the moment.

On My Mind

As I looked up into the sky,
the earth, moon, and stars
must have been aligned
'cause I vowed that I
would be damned if
I would ever let another chick
stay constantly on my mind!
My thoughts are intertwined,
not twisted, but concrete, solid,
Locked, like your locks,
'cause you're a missing link
that I thought I would never find!
It's more than you just being fine ...
you can hold a decent conversation;
it's not all about your body and looks
or about the fancy books
you might have read,
but instead,
it's about your heart and the
thoughts from your head.
You make me think of you
in a different perception,
no misleading, but pure genuine
honesty with no deception.

So, deep down in my heart,
I know that I lied,
'cause I said and I vowed
that I would never let another chick
stay constantly on my mind.
But I close my eyes and picture
those beautiful brown eyes
and see that pretty smile
that lights up the world;
I pray that it could all be mine!
I'd hold you, kiss you, and love
you unconditionally,
always be there for you, and love
you wholeheartedly ...

But all I can do is let the time fly,
hoping one day that you
could possibly be mine.

In the Bed, Missing You

Puffy red eyes,
pillow soaked with tears—
you are so far away, and
I just want you near.
Here!
Close!
By me,
so I can hold you right now.
I'm looking at the ceiling,
wanting you right now!
My vision is blurry …
guess that is from dried-out tears.
My thoughts are heavy.
I'm just trying to get my
heart to adhere!

This long distance is rough;
our situation is tough.
I'm longing for your lips
while missing your touch!
I miss you so much!
Naw, I miss you a lot!
To miss you as well as love you the way I do …
who would have thought?
I want you close by
so I won't have to miss you as much …
and won't have to cry!
I try
to maintain,
doing anything crazy;
I think about you
and restrain
my thoughts, my words,
my heart, my mind.
I just need your soothing voice
to assure me things are fine!
To mess up what we had
is something I wouldn't do.
I'm just crying in the bed,
thinking
about how much I miss you!

Missing You

The pain inside, it runs deep,
real deep,
so deep,
through my veins and bones,
to the point where I can't sleep!
I toss and I turn,
hell, I turn and I toss,
'cause without you right now,
I feel so lost.
Why did you have to leave?
Why did you have to go
away …
so far …
so distant.
There's so much distance;
I'm trying to be patient
but I can't help but be persistent.
For instance,
no one can make me laugh
quite like you,
or make me feel special
the way that you do.
With all this pain and hurt
making me feel the way I do,
I guess in so many words,
I miss you!

Interlude for Elysha

I think of you,
my most beautiful and idolized prize.
You're getting big now, and to my surprise,
you have your own persona and creative mind flow,
and I can't wait till the day you are grown, because
you're going to make an impact on this world somehow,
like you do to me every day, and though we are miles away,
I love you so much, and I'm glad you are my child.
I am just so anxious to see you older, so you can really make me proud.

Best Dreams Are from You

You come to me in my dreams, constantly talking to me …
Daddy, you and Mommy need to stop arguing, y'all acting up,
y'all need to start talking again.
You kiss me on my cheek, look me in my eyes,
whisper in my ear how everything will be all right.
We're in an open field and I'm watching you
doing active things, then you yell out to me,
C'mon, Daddy, come push me in the swings!
I sit up and go along with the plan.
Now I'm looking down at you while you're holding my hand.
It's nothing but peace and serenity in your soul,
and you're an opened, free spirit that can't be controlled.
You're a burst of energy, and I knew then that you
were heaven-sent to me!
And though me and Mommy don't see quite the same,
we both really love you and that will never change!
And just when the feeling is feeling all too right,
I wake up and look around and you're nowhere in sight!
You come to me in my dreams, and it hurts that you're not here,
and it's so many times that I wish you were.
So I close my eyes to dream of a place
where it's just me and you and you wipe the tears from my face,
'cause I know when I wake up
that my heaven-sent angel just helped me make it
through the day!

Heart to Heart

I'm far from perfect.
I'm just an average man.
You're my other side,
and for you,
I will do all that I can.
If I slack,
take me by the hand,
sit me down;
let's draw out a better plan.
I can put my pride to the side
to better not just me,
but us,
Because, whatever you're bringing to me,
I know I can trust!
I respect your input
and what you bring to the table.
I just want you happy,
so I'm willing and able
to make it right.
I'll die trying to make it perfect,
'cause after all you've done for me,
baby, you're worth it!
You mean the world to me,
you deserve it!
We both have gone through heartache
and both have experienced pain,
but we promised each other,
we would not go through that again.
I just wanted to let you know
that, yes I'm your man.
Sometimes I want to just clear the air,
and I hope you understand.
I haven't done anything bad,
so relax and chill.
You can stop pacing back and forth …
be cool, be still.
I'm just telling you how I feel
and what's going on in my heart,
so if there is something that I'm

not doing, we can have a fresh new start.
I think couples need to do that
so there won't be any pressure,
so when they are talking,
it won't seem like some lecture.
Understand where I'm coming from,
'cause I'd rather focus on what we're doing
right, instead of figuring out what went wrong!

Even When I Don't Show It

Your love me for me, in good and bad times,
when I was down on my feet, when I
cheated and lied,
you still stayed by my side
when I said hurtful things and made you cry.
You say encouraging things even when I give you my ass to kiss, and
whoever thought that it would be like this?
I put my pride to the side and say, *Baby I apologize for the times I wasn't
there,*
for the lies and making you cry.
Sometimes I get so caught up in my emotions that I ignore you,
and I really am sorry. So trust me, boo, that when I say you're my world,
I do mean it and I love you.
So I'm just gonna man up, 'cause you deserve it:
I love you, even when I don't show it!

How do I say

I don't know how to say I'm so sorry for all the pain I caused,
'cause you were my everything in our relationship!
I lied and I cheated, always breaking your heart,
putting things before you when you were first from the start.
I took things for granted and brushed off your feelings,
and I couldn't understand why you would blow up, and, shit, hit the
ceiling.
I know I was being selfish and thinking of my own feelings.

I don't know how to say I'm so sorry for each tear I made you cry,
'cause all in all, it was you who was truly by my side.
All of the arguing and fighting just wasn't worth it,
'cause we were so close; now we don't even talk and that don't make no
sense!
Every day wasn't good, but every day wasn't bad;
you were the best thing I messed up that I wish I still had.
I put you through turmoil and messed up situations
when I could have just chilled out, been easy and real patient.

I don't know how to say I'm so sorry for hurting your feelings.
When you wanted lil things out of life, I shattered your dreams and killed
'em!
You wanted the best for us, but I was worried about me,
constantly being selfish and not thinking of the family.
You right, I was a jerk, hanging out late instead of
coming straight home and chilling with you after work.

I know there is nothing that I can say
to stop you from hating me in the worst way.
You've moved on and you're happy; you deserve it.
I just wanted you to know I'm so sorry for hurting you,
'cause you never deserved it!

Inner Conflict

She so damn fine I get caught up thinking about her curves,
and it's plenty of times that I just want to leave to be with you
but I know that thought is absurd!
Pretty ass, lips, and them seductive-ass eyes!
You a cool-ass chick and always down to ride!
We can keep an intellectual conversation and we could hang
out and chill, but I say naw, 'cause I know that would lead
to all kinds of temptation.
See, I already messed up, 'cause I have these thoughts about you,
knowing I shouldn't but damn—what should I do?
I let these thoughts fade out 'cause it's not worth it,
just because we having a hard time, losing you is not worth it!
I took my vows seriously and I'm not about to let nothing
come between you and me!
I fight off this nonsense and try not to do anything drastically,
'cause I love my wife and I would never jeopardize my family!
So what I do now is sit and think about how I first met my wife,
'cause you are my ride or die chick and I love you for life!
I'm not perfect, and I've made plenty of mistakes,
but not having you in my life is something I just couldn't take!
I continue to hustle, strive, and do right for us,
'cause I would never trade in our love for a couple of hours of lust!!

I Will Never Love

I will never love anybody
the way I love you,
but there were just some things
we had to go through.
Our love was tight, but
our bond wasn't there;
we put each other
in situations that simply
weren't fair.
We tried to move on,
but kept coming back
to one another.
We're in two different places,
trying to be strong for one another.
It's a constant battle,
two trying to become one,
but because we loved each other,
we kept trying to hold on.
We both knew that we
had to go our separate ways, but
we're still trying to hold on
and maintain.
We even tried praying
to show each other we
weren't playing!
Somehow that didn't work out;
guess it was meant for us,
to go another route.
My heart is still heavy,
'cause at times I long for you.
I know that we will never be together;
that is why
I will never love anybody
the way I love you!

Broken Heart

I open my eyes slowly.
I can actually see the clouds of smoke,
and the ashes are falling all around me!
I turn to the left and then my right.
I'm in the middle of this disaster,
and there is no one in sight.
My eyes are watery,
my palms are sweaty;
I'm past the stage of denial,
and my heart is heavy!
I don't know what to do
at this very moment.
I don't know what to think;
my thoughts are bare,
more like I'm actually scared
of the unknown.
Many times, I am in control
of my situations,
but this feeling is new,
these are uncharted waters.
How do I regroup?
What steps do I take first?
See, everything has been said!
All the thoughts have been spoken;
we have put everything on the table
and out in the open,
but the pain still hurts,
because this is the day that
my heart was broken!

Right or Wrong

You didn't get me anywhere;
you led me to heartache
and showed me the road to pain.
I tried hard to keep my cool and maintain,
but you hurt me so bad, I damn near
can go insane!

I've never seen you, but I've felt your touch
like a crack fiend with an adrenaline rush.
Sometimes I feel you in my heart; other times
you're in my head.
I see you when you're like an epidemic and you constantly spread.
Sometimes I wish you were a human so
I could beat you to death, 'cause the feelings
I have I wish I never felt.

I don't hate—sometimes I do; most of the time
you're to blame, so tonight it's all on you!
You give me mixed emotions, like I don't care
when I do, and when I do, I really don't, to
the point where sometimes, I will and then
sometimes I won't care about nothing but me
and my feelings, but then you come into effect
and give me healing.
You make me feel strange, like a moody-ass person
whose feelings constantly change.
I don't know if I should be angry or happy
at how you interact in my life,
so I'll always question you,
is loving wrong, or is it right?

Crush

I long for your touch.
When I'm near you,
it's an adrenaline rush.
I'm constantly looking at you
'cause I can't get enough
of your smile—
especially that sexy persona
that makes me blush.
I guess you know
this is more than a crush!

Our connection, for whatever reason,
brought us back together,
However …
a lot of time has passed us by,
but it's still whatever!
You have been through your situations,
I have been through mine.
As long as we communicate and remain open,
everything else will be fine.
I'm just coming at you for real.
I usually don't speak my feelings, but
this is how you make me feel.
You have me stepping out of my element.
I've been longing for you for a while;
I guess you're heaven-sent!
Every since
we started talking,
I guess it was evident
that being around you,
I loved your presence.

CREATIVITY:
Plagues My Mind

Sitting Here Flowing

I'm just sitting here flowing, 'cause half of the things on my mind
y'all really don't be knowing. Got a baby girl in this world and I
love her to death, but I hurt the best thing in the world and left
her by herself. No one sees the hurt or even the cries, 'cause
I hate being alone, so I lie; yeah, I have a lot of chicks on the side,
but it's due to past things that I go through when I don't put down my
pride.
I try to do what's right, but it's so hard; I even go to my knees to call on the
Lord. Help me and my family and friends in good and bad situations.

I'm just sitting here flowing, 'cause it's a lot of things on my mind
y'all really don't be knowing. At times I want to just ski-mask a nigga,
catch someone slippin' and pull the trigga! I get tired of being hurt from
past
relationships; I try to move on, but I can't get past the shit! I've hurt loved
ones
and ones that I cared about; when I could have done one thing, I chose
another route.
I really want them to know that I care and love them, and I wish that there
were a way
that I could show them. My eyes sometimes get teary, 'cause some of the
people I care about fear me! Not in a bad way, but they fear letting me into
their lives, 'cause of some of the decisions I made. If I had a chance I would
let them know that I am *truly* sorry for the hurt and all the pain. I don't
know what's making me even flow like this—
I guess it's a lot on my mind and I'm tired of this shit!

I'm just sitting here flowing, 'cause it's a lot of things on my mind
y'all really don't be knowing—the everyday stress takes over my mind,
makes me want to turn to a life of crime; this life shit is hectic, and at times
when things don't go my way, I get skeptic.

I'm just sitting here flowing, 'cause it's a lot of things on my mind
y'all really don't be knowing ...

Past, Present, and Future

My past is behind me, my present is inevitable, and my *future* awaits!
Some ask where the change came from. I'm just in a different state …
state of my mind, state of cool, state of peace …
sometimes you have to let go of things that are bearing you down,
let go of people that bring you down.
Though mistakes are made, I don't let them dictate or devour me;
I keep pushing on, second by second, minutes, and hourly.
The negative outlook and outcry, I let ride.
My past is behind me, my present is inevitable, and my *future* awaits!
Some ask what's going down. I just say hold on and wait.
The ride has been bumpy, but troubles don't last always.
I continue to prosper and enjoy the wonderful days
Though I don't have all that I want, and I left things behind,
I walk with my head up, 'cause I'm at peace with a different kind of pride.
Thank you to all those who hurt me, left me alone, lied, and cheated me;
those who downplayed me, laughed, talked behind my back, and deceived
me!
You made me stronger, way too strong … 'cause I look at life in a different
light,
and though things aren't always going my way, hey, it's all right!
To those that I hurt, mistreated, and misled,
I apologize for taking your feelings for granted, for making you take on
my ideas when I know that you really couldn't stand it!
I was wrong and selfish; I admit that,
so charge me, not my heart … 'cause I'm on a new beginning,
with a different start
because I'm on a different level, where I'm on a different plateau.
You don't have to believe me, but just look at me, 'cause
I'm just letting you know:
I say this with pride and reluctance, but I don't hesitate
because my past is behind me, my present is inevitable, and my *future*
awaits!

Day at the Bank

In line at the bank,
all that's on my mind is
this money I'm gonna withdraw …
Lady in front of me,
her kids running around
just acting a plum fool!
Guy behind me is on his phone,
talking, actually arguing with whoever
he is talking to …
Three people left before I do all
I need to do—
Maaan, now four guys walk in
at the same time, looking
crazy as hell.
(Laughing to myself) *Man, you stupid!*
Next … I hear the teller call for the next person …
Maaan, finally, almost there.
I have so much to do today
and the only reason I came
to the bank today
was because I thought it wasn't
going to be busy at all today!
Boy, was I wrong!
Out of the blue …
"Everybody get the hell down!
Don't make any sudden moves,
or everybody dies!"
What the hell?
I'm thinking …
How the hell, outta all days,
I come to the bank,
it's the day that I come
and it gets robbed?
Where they do that at?
So my blackness kicks in;
you don't have to tell me but
one time to get on the ground!

Two guys rush the counter!

One is by the door,
the last guy is by me,
yelling, telling everybody
not to move and lay facedown
on the floor!
Great! The nervous guy is by me,
and the lady with the two kids,
one of her sons is saying he got to pee!
My eyes are closed, and I'm praying
that everybody pay attention
and do everything they are saying!
Now, the security dude,
he on the ground trying to maneuver
his weapon!
I'm shaking my head at him,
thinking … *Lord, don't let these dudes catch him!*
I know he trying to protect the bank,
'cause that's his duty …
but security guys and officers
always get shot trying to be the hero
in all movies!

I don't know why
I'm nervous,
but I'm not scared …
I guess it's just a feeling
that I have, it's something in the air.
See, I saw the dudes
when they walked in …
and they gave me a sick
feeling from within!
But I'm not judgmental,
just observant …
and if anything happens to anybody,
they truly won't deserve it!

All we want is this
situation to hurry and be over;
give these dudes what they want,
so this all can be over …
quickly …

In a timely manner ...
I know that this is all over the
police scanner!
You know the news is all over this
breaking news ...
I wonder what these dudes
are going to do!
How are they going to get out of
this bank?
Did they even think?
or plan that through?
Hmmm,
again I think to myself ...
What are these dudes going to do?

By now it really doesn't matter,
'cause whatever is going down,
it's just going to happen,
but I'm tired, and the thought
of the unknown is draining me.
Whoever is coming to defuse
the situation,
I wish they would come
in a hurry!
I guess they have set their demands,
did whatever they had to do,
and met their plans ...
all I know,
this has been an active day,
'cause I never thought
that I would be a hostage in the bank!

Real Bad Night

It's cold outside, and something doesn't feel so right.
I've had a long, bad day at work, and I just want to
forget about this night!
I sit in the driveway to relieve a lil stress,
hoping that when I get in the house it won't be no mess ...
No drama, a clean house ... positive attitudes,
nobody's slick mouth!
I get out the truck and begin to walk
up the stairs ...
I suddenly stop. Something don't feel right!
I can feel it in the air ...
It could be my bad day has me
a little thrown off
'cause I'm aggravated and a little distraught!
Hmmm, what is that shadow? As I think to myself,
I hope nobody out here, 'cause I'm by myself ...
Oh shit!
It's too late ...
I see him lurkin' ...
he's up on me so quick!
I see him smirkin' ...
Bamm! Bamm! Bamm!
That's three rounds ...
My body is hot; now it's cold,
and I hit the ground!
Lord, please don't let me die!
That's what I think ...
I'm still kind of conscious as I lay and cry.
Somebody tried to rob me ...
As I lay on the ground,
he probably thought I was dead, 'cause I'm bleeding bad,
while I lay face down.
But I'm still coherent, and I feel my extremities ...
I just got to play like I'm dead so he can hurry up and leave!
Footsteps are gone ... and it's silent ...
I don't hear nothing, 'cause it's real quiet.
I dial 911 and tell them somebody shot me.
Then I call my dawg and tell him somebody
tried to off me!

Paramedics are there and I see the look in they eyes.
I've lost a lot of blood, but they are surprised
I'm still in good shape, and everything is okay.
But I know I will never, ever forget this day.
My bad day got worse, and in a blink of an eye,
I'm thankful for everything, 'cause that night I could have died!
Now I love different and have a different care …
but to say what else could go wrong on my bad day—
I wouldn't dare!

Love Lost and Gone

I can't believe that you would even lie,
get on the stand and testify
that I was the one to get the demand and supply!
You were supposed to be my dawg, my right hand man; now I wish you
would die!
You were supposed to be my other brotha, and anything that you needed …
I was down to ride!
Now I'm about to be behind these bars
for damn near my whole life,
all because you was jealous
and wanted a piece of my pie.
More like my profit,
maan, shiiit!
You done set me up?
I can't believe this!
I can't even put my hands on you the way I want to!
All I can focus on is dodging these clowns behind bars, and give it to a
nigga if I need to!
To see you walk in the court and point me out
was something I would have doubted!
It is what it is …
right, friend?
Or should I call you the enemy?
I wish you had never befriended me
'cause all the signs was showing that you envied me!
I'm not saying doing what I did was the best, but I did what I did to
provide!
So when the boyz ran up on me with the papers saying I'm indicted …
I just sat still and called my lawyer.
He had already told me I would do some time,
and that the DA had some bullshit charges on me,
but I didn't think it would be coming from a so-called friend of mine!
You can't even look me eye to eye!
You saying we cool,
wiping tears from your eyes,
saying that the folks had you jammed up, and the only way to avoid time
was to put me out and say I was the mastermind!
It's how the game goes!
All my family taken care of, and with the money they straight!

I will do my time, chill and wait
till the release day when they let me out!
Hopefully, for your sake, this game right here,
you get out,
'cause it's going to be a matter of time before we cross paths …
and you better hope I will be a changed man, 'cause you don't want to feel
my wrath!
Feel my rage!
Behind this cage
I'm full of rampage!
I know I'm going to be fine!
Books to keep my mind at ease,
letters and pics from the family,
commissary straight,
still got money in the bank!
Let this be a lesson learned …
that friendship ain't shit!
Friendship is earned,
'cause if a person is jealous
and it comes between you and him,
then you getting burned!

To all my go-gettaz locked down for some so-called friend who pointed a
finger at you, and you had to do the time while he out in your hood with
your girl doing what he do …
remember, what goes around, comes around!

Stars

I'm looking up at the stars, thinking of all the places I would rather be …
'cause I feel all the pressure and stress, and it's eating at me.
I take in so much, but there's no place to give it back,
so I look up at the stars, ease my mind, chill and relax …
I wonder if the stars see that I look at them the way I do,
and that I rely on them to relax my mind when it's things I'm going through.
I'm looking up at the stars and I see one fall in the sky,
and I think to myself, *Do stars really die?*
Do they feel the stress to shine so bright? Twinkle just right?
I wonder if they feel crowded in the sky by themselves,
or if they feel like they want to be by themselves.
I'm looking up at the stars while I'm chilling at the beach;
I feel more calm and at a place of peace.

Day at the Beach

I sit at the beach and just stare at the sky.
I'm alone in this place and no one is by …
by me,
by myself …
is how I'd rather be.
The water splashes hard
against the rocks
as the tide rolls in.
I look down at the clear blue water
and let my mind wander free,
like me writing in the sand,
and the water comes in and
erases my thoughts …
is equivalent to me
ignoring things that bother me,
erasing them and blocking them out.
Coming here has always relaxed me;
it relieves my stress,
so this is where I come to get things
off of my chest.
Some come to relax, some come for pleasure …
I come to chill, be easy, and be down for whatever.
I love coming to the beach,
just to get away …
madness, stress, and things
that go on throughout the day …
throughout the week …
when I'm weak
and feel like I need a break,
just to break
away from everything and everybody.
These are just some of the things
I do to keep life within reach,
so I take my mind off things
with a day at the beach.

In the Elevator

From the thirty-fourth floor down,
all of a sudden,
you step in.
We smile at each other,
With a *how are you* introduction.
Fine … you reply.
Yes, you are, I think to myself.
"That's good," I say,
It's a long way down.
I'll break the ice;
"How was your day?"
An instant smile I see …
My day was stressful and long!
I understand that; mine was, too.
I'm glad to be going home.
She replies, *Me, too,*
and ask me, *So what do you do?*
I break down the job description
to let her know what I do.
She is like, *Wow, you really seem like a real cool dude!*
"Yes, I am, but saying is one thing,
seeing it is another …
'cause, honestly, I'm not the regular type of brother!
I'm laid back and cool,
I like to write, cook now and then,
hang out and shoot pool."
She is like, *That's good to know,*
I didn't know what kind of impression you were under …
I don't always talk to strangers,
but I would love to exchange numbers!
I'm down for that …
I properly introduce myself.
Her name is Brenda.
"If you aren't busy Friday night,
how about we go to dinner?"
She says she can hardly wait.
I smile to myself …
I played it so cool, being myself;
now I have a dinner date …

(ding ding ding)
The elevator door chimes.
I was so tired,
now I have to open my eyes.
See, the real story is,
when I saw her walk in,
I didn't really say nothing,
so I smiled and grinned,
leaned back and dozed off.
I was just so tired and happy to be off.
She looked at me
and said,
Awww, that poor baby is sleepy!
The whole thing was a dream,
and now I'm upset,
'cause I could have said something,
but now there are regrets.
Time to move on.
Don't even know what to say to her;
That is what I get for my missed opportunity
from the fine lady in the elevator!

Dreaming

Beautiful!
Stand right there ...
don't move.
Let me kiss you right here!
It don't matter who is around,
I really don't care!
My hand is in your hair ...
it's blowing in the wind ...
I feel it in the air!
Sexy!
You are that ...
It's so obvious; I didn't even have to state the facts!
Is it true
that we are those opposites that attract?
Never mind that!
Back to business,
back to the topic ...
Back to me and you—
I love you!
Everybody is like, "Stop it!"
Our love, they say, is making them sick.
Loving you, I can't help it!
We go through our ups and downs,
but we still manage.
People see what we have—
I guess they can't stand it.

I see you at a distance;
the closer I get to you,
the farther away you get.
Stop running from me.
You play too much,
see, you make me sick!
I laugh to myself,
thinking you are running away!
Come here!
Baby, don't play ...

You're in my face, and you tell me that you are okay ...

Okay?
I don't really understand
what you are trying to say!
The more my eyes are focusing,
the more you're fading away!

I'm wet!
I don't know if I'm cut or
if it's sweat!
No time to panic,
I'm losing sight of you!
Can't let that happen …
You're so far away!
How did this happen?
I'm yelling out to you,
Baby!
You tell me you're okay!
I hear the sound rumbling;
it's so loud!
It's drowning you out!

I'm focusing, reaching out to you but
you're gone!
Noooooo!
I look up in the air!
God, why did you take her?
This isn't fair!

Honestly!
I open my eyes …
Poof …
Vanished!
Gone!
You were never there!

Beautiful and sexy—
you will always be that to me.
The wet feeling I had
was from the tears from you in my sleep.
We haven't talked in over two years,
but you still mean a lot to me.

I don't know why I'm dreaming of you.
I can't get you out of my mind.
Though we don't talk physically,
you come to me in my dreams,
to let me know you're doing fine.
I don't know how to tell you that
I still think of you,
but whenever you want to talk, come by, if you know what I mean …
Knock on the door
and I'll let you in again in my dream!

Destination: You

Part II

You talked and talked over and over
when I told you that one day
it won't always be text messages
and over the phone conversations.
Now I'm in town,
and you're patiently waiting
to see me face to face,
and maybe try to sneak in a kiss,
'cause you're still wondering
if I have the soft-ass lips!
Now I call you, just to let you know
I'm on the way
and to get directions
so I know where you stay!
Outside your door …
you open the door …
no reason to talk,
we already know what's in store!
You say you diggin' the dreads,
and can you run your fingers
through my head?
Hell, yeah!
You surely can!
But things like that
is going to get you in trouble, ma'am!
Now we face to face,
eye to eye!
You say fuck it!
Now you're kissing me!
Lifting my head up,
my neck,
maaan, you licking me
softly …
slowly …
romantically …
boldly!
Up against the wall …

we still kissing.
Your pants are off,
and now you wishing
that I would take you
by sliding inside.
See, there are two poles ...
one is the one in your room,
and the other is the one I have.
I ain't about to stroke you just yet,
so no need to be mad!
Now you picked up
and I have you in my arms;
up, up, and away!
I have you picked up
while I'm eating you,
yes, against the wall!
You can't squirm away—
hell, you can't even crawl!
You just taking this head game
that I'm giving you
from the wall to the pole in your room.
I know he don't give it to you
the way I do!
On the edge of the bed,
you breathing frantically.
Now I'm stroking you slow ...
you moaning dramatically!
Shhh, bend over, 'cause I know you want it from the back ...
and that spot on your ass,
I know you want it smacked!
I'm picking you up while hitting it from the back,
you saying that you love me,
and you ain't never had it done like that!
I know our situation is complicated,
but you're where my heart is at!
That was just the beginning,
now you want seconds and thirds ...
You always trying to be hard,
you get on my nerves!
But for tonight!
you're mine ...

and you said whatever happens, happens
right?
Bathroom scene …
In the bathroom,
and now you're getting nearer;
Daddy, fuck me from the back,
so I can watch you in the mirror!
Your wish is my command …
so you can melt in my mouth,
and not in my hand …
It won't stop there,
we've got all night …
You said you needed some real loving;
I'm the one to do it right!
Open back up, so I can eat you until
I get tired …
My tongue is strong!
I'm amped up and wired!
It happened again …
an all nighter.
Trying to be hard …
trying to be a fighter …
got you tapping out …
hanging up your belt;
now you're gonna retire!
I guess I won this round
of me coming to town …
breaking you off and putting it down!
So, until next time,
close your eyes
so you can replay this scene
again and again …
'cause the more you think about it,
the more you will want to be more
than my friend!

Strip Show

See, I been looking at you all night,
you doing the damn thing,
and you looking so right!
Body so tight …
eye to eye …
nothing but passion,
not a word said,
but we feel each other's compassion!
It's hot in here!
We're past the stage of lust;
going at it all night,
we're past the stage of dusk!
You shaking and moving,
I'm chilling and cruising …
loving what you doing.
Shhhh …
don't stop moving!
This is a first for both of us;
you have me so turned on,
I'm about ready to bust!
I'm trying to contain myself,
but you have me ready to let go.
you poppin' it fast,
then turning your hips
all so slowly!
Your body is so sexy,
even your beads of sweat
are looking right.
You have damn near nothing on,
and it's looking so nice!
Licking your lips,
you running your tongue
up and down my neck.
I'm waiting for your kiss.
You work your way back down,
and I'm thinking,
Ahhhh man, you doing me like this?
I'm not even going to complain.
I'm enjoying your show.

Keep holding me tight baby!
Don't let go!
You giving me the red light special ...
my own personal strip show!
I have to admit,
I didn't think you was even
going to put it down like this!
You need to be on stage,
'cause the way you moving tonight,
I know you would get paid!
I'm not saying that
in a disrespectful way;
I'm just saying that your performance
had me so turned on
I couldn't help
but go along
with what you were doing.
All my attention was on you,
from the way that you moved
to everything that you were doing!
Thank you, momma!
I enjoyed my show,
but you need to surprise me again
with another strip show!

Never Ever

We just got into a heated argument last night; as I awake, you have your back to me, and strangely, I'm not mad, 'cause when I woke up, you were still beautiful to me. I didn't quite understand it, or even quite get it … *Hmmm,* I thought to myself, *Damn, Etrec; what is it?* Then I smiled to myself; I already knew what the answer was! I couldn't even stay all that mad, 'cause finally I was in love! And I've been in love before, but it hurt me so bad that I tried to block it out by staying so mad. But without a doubt, I couldn't block it out, so I put my guard down and took another route! I decided to give it a chance but I didn't know it was so intense—that you would have me all in love, and to me it didn't make sense. I knew my feelings for you were strong to the point where we could move in together, but I didn't know it would sneak up on me like this! Ten minutes have gone by and you haven't rolled over yet, but I'm just looking at you sleep; you look so peaceful, you look so discrete! I kiss you on the cheek, smiling to myself. I whisper in your ear and tell you I love you! I go take a shower, ready to start my day and end our little feud; ready for you to meet me in the shower 'cause I love seeing you nude! As time goes by, I feel something ain't right, 'cause you still in the same position that you were in last night. "Get up, sleepy head," I say as I shake your shoulders, but you ain't budging and your body is way colder than it usually is … Now I'm in a frantic state of mind, 'cause you haven't moved at all. At a drop of a dime, I call 911 'cause you're not even breathing, and I can't get a pulse! I'm trippin' and screaming, "Baby! Please get up!" But you're not moving, and the thought of you gone—I'm losing … my mind, my cool! The EMTs are there, asking me what happened; I'm frantic and scared. I tell them the whole story of what went down and took place. They take the mask off you and look each other in the face. I know it's not a good look, and the pain is piercing my heart and soul 'cause of what I'm about to be told … "Mr. White, I'm so sorry, there is nothing we could do." I just feel this eerie feeling all out of the blue. She must have had a condition to where she couldn't breathe; my baby laid down after a petty argument and died in her sleep! I never got the chance to tell you I loved you!

Moral of the story, tomorrow is never promised to anyone. Tell that one whom you love or think you love, that you love them!

One-Way Conversation

Part I

I just walked through the door.
You come from the room and slam the door abrupt.
What's wrong, baby?
You like *What the fuck?*
I'm thinking to myself, hmmm, so I say, "What?"
You say, *I saw you at the bar, talking to that slut!*
Baby, let me explain …
but you not letting me talk.
You slapping me like you crazy, so
before we fight, let me chill out and just walk.
Where the hell you going now? To go be back with that bitch?
F— you punk, 'cause you think you slick!
I ain't done nothing! This ain't what you think …
Shut up! I don't want to hear it, I saw that broad you was talking to in pink!
Baby!
Whatever, you're wasting your breath!
What you thought you saw, you're taking out of context!
No, I saw what I saw, you just trying to run game,
talking about you working late, when you out playing!
I gave you the world and put up with all your bullshit,
and this is how you do me—I can't believe this shit!
If you let me speak for a minute, I can explain the whole situation,
and you can determine for yourself,
if I'm really playing!
Please! Just leave 'cause the sight of you is making me sick!
I hate you! I swear! I'm nauseous and sick …
Maan!
Please! Shut up and go! Before I do something I'll regret.
I'm hot as hell, and I'm starting to sweat!
Fine! Have it your way; I'm about to be out!
I'm not in the mood to scream and shout.
You have put up with my shit and been there from the jump!
I wouldn't do you any ol' kind of way and do none of that stuff!
But when you ready to talk, hit me on the hip …
Yeah, whatever, just leave, leave me alone, and I mean that shit!

(A couple of hours later …)

Maan, this is unbelievable; this is all too funny,
and when the truth comes out …
you gonna be looking like a dummy!
Yeah, I did meet a chick at the bar,
but it was my cousin …
she was on the other side of the bar!
I told her to meet me, 'cause I needed her opinion …
Something was on my mind and I needed her
to help me with a decision.
You woke me up one morning,
talking about this dream,
so I had my cousin go with me to make your
dream come true and surprise you
with an engagement ring!
I wanted a female's perspective and a female's point of view
of how something so beautiful
would look good on you!
But I didn't plan on you coming out; matter of fact,
I didn't think you would come to the spot
where we would hang out at!
So, I'm wrong 'cause I covered the truth,
but I wasn't doing nothing wrong; it was
a surprise, all for you!
But that's what happens with a perceived notation,
and this is what you get in a one way conversation …

Operation: Love Overdose

Now what we have here is a typical example of miscommunication,
So this situation is on high alert.
Grab the team, 'cause we are in serious need of deliberations.
Put all of the drama to the side, 'cause we are going to need full concentration.
Both parties have agreed, so there is full cooperation.
Operation: Love Overdose is operational.
So, here is the situation:
Subject #1… We will call him Mr. Elusive …
Subject #2 is his wife; her code will be Mrs. Executive …
Their tactical love strategy has been deemed stupid!
So we got the high alert; our code name will be Cupid!
It seems that their love was on the rocks and in doom, so they called Cupid
and asked us to prepare the situation room …

Subject #1, Mr. Elusive, has been in his own world, not really spending time with his wife.
After reviewing the paperwork, we find serious signs of neglect. No time for one another!
When they talk, there is no interest
or even respect!
This subject is about himself, from what I can detect.
Subject #2, Mrs. Executive, is all about her job and her work; she wants her husband to do everything that she wants, and when he doesn't agree, she gets mad and her feelings get hurt.
This is controlling and she is trying to realize her worth.
As Cupid, we must break down each subject's matter, see what's going on.
How can we make them happier?
Half of you take subject 1…
The other half will take subject 2 …
Here is a list of things that you all should do …
Evaluate them to see where their hearts are …
Both parties have agreed to cooperate; so there shouldn't be a problem with that.
This relationship will probably be the hardest by far …
It is up to us to make sure they don't fall apart!

{Cupid team with subject 1}

Mr. Elusive, thank you for being open and cooperative … after talking to you, here is a short analysis of what we came up with:

Your wife means the world to you; you just got comfortable and complacent.

These are mere facts, so just face it!

We can help you rekindle the flames;
there's no need to be embarrassed or ashamed!

This happens all the time, and here are some pointers we want you to use if you don't mind.

Take your wife out to the beach, tell her to sit down on the sand, look her in the eyes while you let the water hit her feet, then start rubbing on her feet.

Now, she might look at you kind of strange at first, but keep going, I promise it won't hurt to rub her feet and massage her ankles, tell her you love her and that she is so special. Pick her up and her let piggyback to the car. It will be the best time you all had thus far!

Take her to a romantic dinner, tell her she is your prize and you will do anything to win her.

Go back to the house and put on some slow music; grab her by the hand. Enjoy the music and begin to slow dance …

She is going to look at you and think, *What has gotten into him?*

Tell her that the answer to that question is her!

Now make your way to the bedroom and dim the lights; tell your wife you love her and slowly make love to her all night!

Take these steps and do as we say, and things will gradually change …

{The other half of the Cupid team with subject 2}

Mrs. Executive, hello; thank you for letting us review your case.

We can get you back to the point of being back in love, if you just do what we say.

You have been putting your job before the person you lay with.

It's been a meaningless process with the one that you stay with.

You have all the time for your job, but not even a lil time for your mate;
I'm just reading all the signs and info, and that's what it clearly states.

So we are here to help you get the love back.

We are going to give you some things to do; hopefully, you don't have a problem with that!

Tell your husband to clear his schedule, 'cause tonight, you are going to do something special!

Take him to the park and listen to some jazz. Sit down and enjoy each other, have some drinks and laugh. You take him out to dinner, but you pick up the tab.

He is going to look at you like, *What's gotten in to you?*

Just wink at him and reply, *I love you, boo!*

Now, make your way back to the house; when you get in good, look at him and tell him that you are glad he is your spouse.

Tell him to take off everything and be as quiet as a mouse, 'cause when you come out of the bathroom you're going to show him some things that are going to make him drop his mouth!

Take your time, 'cause he is going to be like, *What's going on?*

Then surprise him with a naughty nurse outfit on!

You will have to step out of your element, but it will be worth every cent.

Whisper in his ear all night and tell him how you feel, then wait until the next morning and tell him that everything you said, you meant!

You can't go wrong with the advice we gave you; the rest is on you to figure out which route you want to do.

Now, we have all parties in the situation room, and from the looks of things, the situation is no longer in gloom! You two just realized that love is an everyday thing.

You can play or do whatever you do to keep it from a fling.

I see the look of feeling stupid is no longer a feeling as things seem.

I thank everyone involved, especially the Cupid team!

We did a job well done and this situation is now closed, thanks to our tactical warfare, aka Operation: Love Overdose!

Humble

It's nothing but gun shots outside my door.
I don't know what's in store;
I wish Daddy was here.
Maybe he would move us to a better place,
or hold me tight,
wipe the tears from my face!
I just want to go outside sometimes and play,
but it's too many gun fights outside,
so outside isn't safe!
Mommy does the best she can;
I just wish I could lend her a helping hand,
so we can move somewhere where it's quiet and peaceful
so we can all go to sleep and be at ease!
I love to play basketball, but glass surrounds the court.
Instead of playing there, I play in the driveway
on the basketball goal my uncle bought.
I'm just tired of living in this horrible area;
God, if you hear me, please can you spare us?
I ask for help …
I pray every day …
I want things to be different …
In every way!
Not much to do …
Not much to say …
These are the things that I see, I feel,
these are some of my sightings.
I don't complain,
so I put it in writings!
It soothes my mind
and takes away my stress.
This is the best way I can relax!

Silence Is Golden

Thank you for doubting me, my skills, and my abilities.
You have made me more determined with the will and desire.
Quite actually, you have fueled my fire.
I had been on my high horse with accolades and recognitions,
highest praise from my teammates, and honorable mention.
Some way, I lost sight of the bigger picture, doing whatever it took
just to be a winner.
But I was a winner whether we won or lost, leaving it all on the field no
matter the cost.
You stated that we were underachievers
and that you didn't care what we did,
but as soon as we went in a different direction, you're the one acting just
like a kid!
E-mails here and blogs there, all these silly postings ...
thinking that you really hurt us, you're bragging and boasting.
To your demise; surprise! I continue to grow; I don't have to show you
what's in store, I'm going to let my play show!
You can keep talking all that you are, saying that and this, 'cause the next
time you see me on the field, the things I'm going to do, I promise you will
be sick!
I'm going to be a gentleman and even shake your hand, 'cause I know
after I leave your presence, you will be pissed, shaking your head, saying,
"Damn!"
So again, thank you for doubting me, my skills, and all my abilities,
because you fueled my fire and brought the best back out of me!

EMOTIONS:
These Thoughts, These Feeling

It's Not Fine

It's late, and while you holding me tight,
Something ain't right,
'cause I'm thinking about her
and not you tonight.
She is on my mind heavy.
Though she wanted to settle down,
I simply wasn't ready,
so it comes into my head
while I'm trying to sleep with you.
This feeling is horrible and I just
don't know what to do!
Do I wake you up to let you know?
I think to myself, and say, *Hell, no!*
It's something I don't want
you to think about,
and before I go that route,
I will close my mouth.
I can't figure this out.
Why are you on my mind?
I promise, this is going to
take some time.
But in due time, I'll go back
to sleep, like everything is fine.

Eye Opener

I loved you so much, but I took things for granted;
now you're gone,
doing your own thing …
and sometimes I can't stand it!
You meant the world to me,
but I just didn't see
that the things I was doing
were all about me!
Our love was one of a kind,
sensual and genuine.
I think we could have been okay
if we would have put in the time.
I can't take back the hurt,
none of the arguments,
which makes me sick
'cause I see what you were worth!
My best friend is gone;
I don't have no one to blame …
I put this on myself …
and it's my fault that I feel alone!
Sometimes I think about it all,
and I chill out and sympathize,
'cause all in all, I was the one wrong
and for that I truly apologize!

From my point of view,
it's my fault we are through,
and all I can do is move on
to be a better dude.
Again I'm sorry
for all that pain that I caused,
'cause never in my heart and wildest dreams
did I ever mean to do you wrong.

Looking at You, Looking at Me

I'm looking at you,
you looking at me;
I'm wondering what
you're wondering,
you sucking your teeth
mumbling and uttering
feelings of despair.
We looking at each other
as if we don't even care!
Is it the feeling in the air?
Do we try to maintain things?
Is this something we can bear?
Do we love each other?
I ask myself that each day.
Where are we going wrong? Is this the point when we walk away?
I'm tired of the bickering and the pointless conversations …
talking isn't helping us with this situation!
Still,
I'm looking at you,
you looking at me;
I'm wondering what
you're wondering.
Will we continue to be
each other's half, each other's bond, or do we just quit what we are doing
and simply move on?
Is the love really there, or is the love truly gone?
Are we meant to be together?
Is this where we belong?
So many questions, yet there aren't any answers,
you looking like, *He makes me sick,*
While I'm like, *I can't stand her!*
Amazingly,
nothing has really been said.
I'm looking at you,
you looking at me;
I'm wondering what
you're wondering .
Maan, I can't keep doing this;
I'm going to bed!

Apart

I want to cry but I don't know what to do
'cause the feelings I have for you
are through.
No more me and you …
It's apparent,
us being apart,
I know I'm not gonna stand it,
but it's best that we go
our separate ways
'cause I'm cutting all the bullshit
to the side …
starting today!

All the energy, all the time …
The leading me on, all the lies!
You could have been straight up,
but you didn't choose that route
'cause you got caught up
with your foot in your mouth!
It's okay, 'cause time heals all wounds.
I have to leave you alone,
because I'm being consumed!
Things were doomed …
and I already knew,
but I tried to hang on,
'cause I really love you!

I love you enough to leave,
and instead of hanging on …
I will let you be!
There will be no more arguing,
ripping out each other's heart …
though I love you more than words can say,
it's best that we be apart.

Farewell

I asked you, *If I give you my heart,*
will you break it?
You said no,
but the things in my heart
are telling me to go!
See, things you tell me,
I constantly second guess,
so deep down inside,
I know it's best that I left.
This time I'm gone and
there is no looking back.
I avoided a broken heart—
but there is a crack,
'cause part of me thought
you would actually change,
but once again,
with you,
it's the same old thing!
Now I know that you would
think that I would fuss and fight,
but that's pointless,
'cause I'm at a new place in my life.
I've given you time after time,
and chance after chance,
but the way we are going,
I know we would never last.
Yes, I love you with all my heart,
but I'd rather find someone who
will love me for me,
and have a brand new start.
So farewell,
good-bye.
I'm sorry it's like this,
but I have to follow my heart,
'cause it never lies!

Nothing's Changed

You saying that you committed and that you love me for life,
you want what we used to have, and you will do whatever to make it right,
but you still talking to the same dudes that got us to this point the first
time,
so here you go again with all the lies!
Why did I try?
Fooled again …
Right! What a surprise!
Three strikes, you're out, so leave me alone!
Maan, just ride …
I don't care about your tears,
so you can leave and wipe your eyes.
It's nowhere to hide.
Great! Now all my friends know;
I'ma turn off all phones 'cause I don't want to hear all the *told you so's*.
I really can't be mad; it's my fault, I suppose.
Back to the drawing board. That's not a route I really want to go,
but after this time I have to take things slow.
You don't have to call and check to see if I'm okay.
There's nothing for us to do anymore, and there's nothing else to say.
I gave you chance after chance, time after time.
Nothing but the best of me—all I got was your lies!
This is the last time we will ever talk;
because of you, all your ties have been cut off.

I'd Rather

I'd rather be on my own
'cause I feel all alone,
and the thought of love again …
that feeling is gone!
I'd rather be by myself
'cause there is no one else
I feel I can turn to for help
to ease my soul;
I've come a long way,
but my heart has turned cold.
My attitude is horrible,
and my mood is savage—
at least that's what
I've been told.
I'd rather be asleep
than looking at the clock,
wondering why
you do me the way you do?
I'm caught in your lies.
I'd rather be on my own
'cause I feel alone,
and the thought of us together—
those thoughts are far fetched
and gone!

Officially Through

I heard all that you said,
and even how you mean it.
Now, were you being for real?
Or was I a convenience
to some of your needs
or some of your wants,
replacing loves that are gone,
people you've lost?
I don't know what it is
that has me feeling this way,
ready to leave.
I'm in no contentions
and it's some real genuine
people who want to be with me,
so I'm not in to the competition…
Now I don't question
if you love me,
because I know that you do,
it's just some unexplainable things
that you do!
You say you love me to death
and you'd never hurt me,
that you will always
be by my side,
and that you would never desert me,
that you're sorry for what you did,
and how you wish
you could change the past
and the pain that I feel,
how you wish you could take it back.
See, your mouth says one thing
but your actions show another.
There's no need to look amazed
when I say that it's over!
See, I know way more
than you think I know.
I'm just too cool to
ever let my actions show!
See, your other out of town dudes—

mmmm–hmmm, I know about
them too!
It's really a shame
that you trying to be slick;
really ain't your game!
Here's a new game
that I think you should play.
It's called be honest to yourself.
You should try it one day!
But you be easy;
Continue to do you,
because this be the last
time we ever talk,
'cause this time, we are really through!

That Shit

To say we weren't always going to be together—
you couldn't have paid me to say that shit!
And to think that we are no longer together—
man, I can't believe this shit!
We've been friends forever and now we don't even talk—
this is crazy shit!
Wasted our friendship
on some old petty shit!
Making me pick up the pieces and move on,
like, damn, that's that bullshit!
Wondering to myself, how can I go on without you?
I'll be damned, how am I gonna do this shit?
Knowing that you with my friend doing things,
thinking to myself how they gonna do this shit?
To have you calling me now saying that you want me,
'cause ol' buddy you was dealing with is a piece of shit!
Now I am content; I've moved on.
My ol' girl ain't having that shit!
I'm sorry it's the way it is, but be easy 'cause
I ain't hearing none of this shit!

Imagination Running Wild

You got me upside down, head first, with a migraine so bad
that I'm about to burst. You ask me a thousand questions—
damn, I can't think straight! In due time I can get to you, so
can you just wait?
Your impatience is killing me like some weeds to a rose bush,
and I can mess all this up with a bump or a push. You hold me tilted,
sometimes straight up; you wash me with others and mess everything up,
so I'll leave your imagination running wild—would you ever think
that I'm this ink flowing from this pen?

Untitled III

The thought of you, I try to put out of my mind.
Why can't I do it? Is it because of all the time
we spent, the time that we had.?
I don't quite know, I don't understand.
I see your face and I try to block you out.
My emotions inside sometimes make me want to shout.
Though you did what you did, I know it's not hate.
Just the thoughts that I have, I just wish I could erase!
I wish we could talk and try to clear the air,
but we have other relationships and to them it wouldn't be fair!
At times I don't really care ...
I get ready to call, but my mind says don't dare!
A love gone! Friendship is like it never existed.
We don't even talk and now we're so distant!
I'll be the first to admit my faults
for all the wrongdoing and breaking your heart ...
but for it to be this way, I still don't think is right,
but what can I say, guess that's part of life ...
so I just move on, trying to figure what to do,
knowing that we will never be together, all because of you!

Drama

I sit down and wonder how we even got to this point.
Hmmm, I wonder ...
Feels like yesterday when we were sitting on the couch
looking at each other, crying our problems out.
Wow ...
Look at us now.
We don't know the when and can't figure out the how!
All we have is our past and we can't even hold on to that.
Matter of fact ...
it's something wrong with that!
See, I'm always gonna love you, be cool with you, and that will never
change,
and some of our problems—I am to blame!
But you can't put all that mess on me,
see ...
You have been part of the problem too.
You haven't made things easy!
We both have been at each other's throat.
It doesn't make things right or wrong; that's why I take another approach
to smooth things out and make things better ...
but when I try to talk to you it's always,
Whatever.
Arguing with you is no longer in the plans,
'cause I'm on to better things, while trying to be a better man!
I agree to disagree, but this time I'm through ...
'cause I refuse to go through all this drama with you!

Changes

It was supposed to be me and you forever,
then you go do some dumb shit that makes me
can't stand you forever!
However …
I keep things real,
I weather the storm
whether my mind is right,
or whether my heart is torn.
I broaden my horizons
and keep pushing on,
erasing all the memories,
from you all that did me wrong.
Whenever I think of you,
I feel deception and deceit,
and when I close my eyes,
you trifling and a cheat!
I can go on and on
but bashing ain't me …
I'll keep my cool and if you all
happen to see me …
do me a favor—
act like you don't know me!

Better Off Without You

I didn't see us getting to this point.
A lot of times I'm so confused,
I don't know what to do.
Because deep in my heart I know
that I'm better off without you.
We have an extensive history,
a memorable past,
but us being cool is just something,
that won't last.
We've grown apart and taken on
two different paths.
The more we are around each other,
the more we clash!
You even put somebody ahead of me,
and I didn't even get mad about it.
As long as you were happy,
I was glad about it.
You don't feel the same way about me
as I do about you,
so I know it's best that I don't
cross paths with you.
I never wanted this to happen, but its
always been in my face
that you have always cared about you,
and things don't matter as long as they
go your way!
You were supposed to be my best friend,
but you were envious,
and to be quite frank,
you were selfish and real jealous!
I could go on and on, but
bashing just ain't me,
so I always hope for the best for you,
but I have to cut ties
'cause I can't keep going through this with you.
We will always be friends and always be cool,
but I'm better off without you!

I'm Not Feeling Right

I'm not feeling right,
uh–huh,
not at all.
It don't have nothing
to do with this alcohol
I'm drinking,
not sipping,
cup under halfway.
I'm about to just
take to the head
'cause I'm wishing
I never talked to you,
looked at you,
met you!
I don't hate you,
but I dislike you!
True!
What do I do?
What do I think?
What should my
thought process suggest?
I've been honest
about everything;
opened my heart
and confessed!

I'm not feeling right,
uh-huh,
not at all,
not even a lil bit;
I wish I was drunk
so I wouldn't be
thinking about this shit!
My thoughts are aligned,
but my heart is
not in tune.
So do I chill
and let time heal
these wounds?

I'm confused!
Auuughhhh, you make me sick!
I'm supposed to be asleep,
not writing or thinking
about this shit!
I'm not feeling right,
uh-huh,
not at all.
My thoughts and heart
can't take it no more,
so I'm calling it a night!

When Saying I'm Sorry Isn't Enough

When saying I'm sorry isn't enough, what do you do? Give up?
Quit? Step your game up or throw the towel in? Do you admit your faults
and try to make a change, or keep doing what you're doing and keep
playing the same ol' games? Being committed is so hard to do, but
through all the pain, I'm still with you.

When saying I'm sorry isn't enough, what do you do? Do you
put up or shut up? Keep trying your luck to bust a nut? Hmmm …
Tick, tick, tick … times up! Now you're lonely and sorry, 'cause
saying I'm sorry wasn't enough!

Life ... Hmmmm ... I wonder

Maybe God wants us to meet a few wrong people before
meeting the one so that when we finally meet the right person,
we will know how to be grateful for that gift.

When the door of happiness closes, another one opens, but
often we look so long at the closed door that we
don't see the one that has been opened for us.

The best kind of friend is the kind we can sit
on the porch and chill with, never say a word, and
then walk away feeling like it was the best
conversation we ever had!

It's true that we don't know what we've got
until we lose it, but it's also true that we
don't know what we have been missing until it arrives.

Giving someone all your love is never an assurance
that they will love you back! Don't expect love in return;
just wait for it to grow in their heart, but if it doesn't,
be content it grew in yours.

It only takes a minute to get a crush on someone,
an hour to like someone, a day to love someone, but
it takes a lifetime to forget someone.

Don't go for looks; they can deceive. Don't go for wealth; even
that fades away. Go for someone who makes you smile, because
it takes one to make a dark day seem bright. Find the one who
makes your heart smile!

May you have enough happiness to make you sweet, enough
trials to make you strong, enough sorrow to keep you human,
enough hope to make you happy! Always put yourself in others
shoes; if you feel it hurts you, it probably hurts the other person too!

The happiest of people don't always have the best of everything,
they just make the most of everything that comes their way. Happiness
waits for those who cry, those who hurt, those who have searched, and those

who have tried, for only they can appreciate the importance of people who have touched their lives …

Life … hmmmm … I wonder!

My Friend

See, what's funny is when we were young, we had a crazy crush on each
other,
smiles here and there, flirting, but never really saying much to each other.
You would always be on my mind, like, *I'm digging this chick; maan, she
fine!*
But I would never really say much … I wanted to …
I was too busy playing tough!
And one day, outta the blue, you're gone!
I felt real bad 'cause it was more than you that was gone,
it was your presence, 'cause I was used to it,
and I thought to myself, *Damn, Etrec you blew it!*
An opportunity, 'cause at the end, you were still my friend,
and one day you were there, and then you were gone in the wind!
I never told you that I liked you …
or that I couldn't wait to come outside just to be next to you!
Time elapsed and we went our separate ways …
but there wasn't a time when I didn't think about you each day.
I wondered where you were or what you were doing …
if you were in school or which career you were pursuing …
and then all of a sudden, you're back in my life,
and I think to myself that's all right,
'cause we had a bond was stronger than we knew,
'cause we both was on each other's mind, outta da clear blue …
So thank you for taking the time to find what was missing,
a friendship that never died, despite the distance …
and though you do your thing and I'm doing mine …
I'm glad my friend is okay and doing fine.
You still my lil crush, but most of all my friend,
and I will always be here for you, always till the end!

Untitled IV

I'm not the type of touchy-express my feelings type guy,
and because I don't touch you all the time, there's no need to wonder why.
Is he diggin' me,
Is he feeling me,
Maan, is he even into me?
Yes to all three …
I'm kinda of unique.
If you didn't see
I can look into your eyes and already see so much,
that there was already feeling there,
without the first touch!
I like you for you.
I know you thinking,
Can you go more in depth?
Yep …
Here we go, after I take this deep breath:
See, things you are used too,
I really don't do,
but that doesn't mean I'm not feeling you!
I'm down to earth, the type to just go with the flow,
and though you're not used to the word no,
it don't matter to me; I still take things slow.
Don't question how I feel,
'cause for real,
you already know the deal.
I like where we're headed,
and even if nothing came out of this,
I wouldn't regret it.
I still would have a place for you in my heart,
and though the distance has us apart,
we are still close,
our own bond that nobody knows …
so never doubt my emotions
'cause I will never send you through the motions!
Surprise …
I can see the look in your eyes …
'cause now you're next to me, mesmerized.

The World Would Seem Shallow

The world would seem so shallow if I didn't have you in it,
no me without you; I couldn't imagine it, and no me without
your love; I couldn't handle it.
I would probably dismantle shit, go crazy and imagine
your face and picture us in a place where we could

just chill and I could erase any doubt in your mind
that I would ever be the one to hurt you, mistreat you,
lead you astray, 'cause in the long run I want to see you in
a pretty white dress on that special day.

The world would seem so shallow if I didn't have you in it.
I can't fake it, front it, or even pretend it.
You mean more than the world to me,
and I know sometimes I don't show it, and
sometimes I just fly off at the mouth and just blow it,
but I care for you and each word I said is meant,
'cause the world would seem so shallow if I didn't have
you in it!

I'm Thinking

I'm thinking about your
beautiful eyes ...
I'm thinking about your
beautiful smile ...
I'm thinking about your
pretty face
that puts a smile on my face
'cause thinking about you,
honestly, helps me get through my day!
There's nothing to say,
I just want to think about you
and all of the little things you do!
I think about your kisses
and how you greet me when you wake up,
or how you smile and wink at me
when you first wake up.
I think about how you'll be in the bathroom
getting ready for work for over an hour,
or how sexy you look
when you get out of the shower.
I think about that look
that you get when you are turned on.
I love that look you give me
when we getting it on!
I think about how you love me for me,
and how you're down to earth,
making you and me
a family!
I think about you all day every day.
I think about the things you do
and all the things you say.
All in all,
I love thinking about you
'cause, sometimes,
it's the best thing
that I love to do!

Emotions

Unexplainable emotions,
argumentative and moody,
indecisive,
picky and choosey,
hormones up and down,
your feelings are off the chart;
from the way you are looking,
something is on your heart.
It's heavy on your mind.
I wish you would talk to me,
at least to let me know you're fine.
You're crying but you won't
talk to me.
Whatever it is, please, baby,
talk to me!
Whatever it is, it's not that serious,.
It's driving you crazy and making you delirious!
I notice that you really
don't have an appetite lately.
I'm starting to put two and two together;
are you pregnant?
Are we having a baby?
You looking at me crying,
telling me maybe.
Maybe?
That's a yes or no, baby …
you saying that your cycle
is late and that's why
you have been acting crazy!
That's understandable;
all you had to do
was tell me …
talk to me,
let me know something!
You hiding the most important thing from me—
that makes me feel like I'm nothing
to you
or for you,
'cause that's something

I thought you wouldn't do.

The truth is out now, finally.
I'm excited about a family possibility.
We both need to know
if we are adding on to our family tree,
so I will give you time
to find out what's going on …
I will patiently wait
to figure out if we are
going to have a daughter or son!

While You Sleep

I'm rubbing on your forehead while I'm kissing you on your cheek.
You look so beautiful to me; you're at peace while you sleep.
You're wrapped up in the silk sheets and I'm just admiring the scene.
I have the biggest grin on my face 'cause you belong to me.
I just sit in the chair and stare at you for the rest of the night,
amazed at where we are at this point of our life.
So many times I have taken you for granted,
To the point where you were out of my life and I simply couldn't stand it.
Love will overcome any obstacle that stands in its path; that's why I'm up
looking at you as I laugh.
It's not in a funny way,
more in surprise
that after all we have been through, you are still in my life,
still in my thoughts, still in my head …
our love is still alive and not dead!
I rub your shoulders as you turn over and you're looking at me.
Shhh, don't say a word, baby, just go back to sleep.
Let me enjoy the view—more like let me enjoy you as you sleep,
because looking at you sleep is so beautiful to me.

Explanation

Our arguments are childish; they are petty.
Let's be real with one another; are we really ready
for a lifetime commitment and to share each other's heart …
to love one another till death do us part?
If any of those questions have you in dismay,
then we should talk before our wedding day.
I just want to make sure we're on the same page,
'cause all of the pettiness is pushing me away.
I come to you in an open-hearted way
just to make sure this is the route we both want to take.
Please think about the decision you want to make,
so we can figure out which action to take.
No matter what choice you make, I still love you.
This is just something that we have to do!

Realization

Even though you hurt me and made me mad to the highest point of
pissitivity,
I knew that it could never be
that you were better off without me.
Things were hazy and unclear
but now you finally see
that you were visiting the place you were
and where I am is home.
That's where you ought to be.
Now, if I'm wrong, hell, disagree!
But you reading this, smirking,
so I know you agree.
Things were done wrong but
I know it wasn't intentionally.
None of that really matters,
'cause I still love you for you,
and you love me for me.
If things go wrong, at
least trust in me!
Failure to communicate could have
been fixed easily
to where you didn't have to make these
changes so drastically.
The past is in the past so we can
leave it behind us and do things naturally,
systematically,
spur of the moment,
or romantically!
'cause you back home now,
and we're finally a family.

The Trust Issue

You tell me to open up and let you in my world …
It's not that I don't love you; it's just the things I have gone through …
It's the things I have to deal with it, so it doesn't have anything to do with you;
Though deep down I know it's affecting you.
I told you I have trust issues!
So you might be telling me the truth about something,
but in my head, I might not believe you.
I know that things are hard, but my heart is scarred,
so I ask for patience. I understand if you can't take it.
I even understand if you didn't want this relationship anymore,
'cause if you felt somebody could give you what I couldn't, I'm quite sure
that taking another path is what you had in store;
in other words, that's what you had in mind.
It's just that it feels like we are just flying by,
like you biding your time.
I'm not going to change overnight, but if you give me some time,
I promise things will be all right.
I don't mean to hurt your feelings and I don't mean to hurt your heart.
I know the way I'm acting is tearing you apart.
I'm sorry for the situation, not for how I have been acting.
It's just things in my past that have me reacting
to things you say and things you do,
so instead of shutting down, I'm just being up front and communicating
with you.
Please excuse me and please excuse my broken heart.
I know that you are not the one who tore it apart.
You are the one who is trying to heal it; I know you are trying to protect it
and let nobody steal it. You're trying to mold it, hold it, uplift it,
and uplift me, and all I'm asking is that you give me time to be the man
that I can be!

Thoughts of Law Abiding

Can I strip you
while I kiss you,
as soon as you walk
through the door?
Feel your body
in my hands,
while my tongue explores?
Look you in your eyes,
tell you that you are
so beautiful!
I don't care about
none of your flaws.
To me you are suitable.
Can I pick you up
while we kissing,
and walk you into
our bedroom and lay
you down slowly
while we are
still kissing?
Whisper in my ear
what you need and
what's been missing.
Can I whisper in your ear
to close your eyes
while I kiss you from
head to toe,
massage your body,
rub you real nice and slow.
Go into the bathroom;
there is a bubble bath
with rose petals
that awaits you—
just something to put
a smile on your face,
to let you know,
I appreciate you.
The things you do
don't go unnoticed,

even when you think I'm
not paying attention or being focused.
Actually I am,
I just have my way of showing it.
This is just something
to say how I feel about you,
the things I like doing for you,
and another way to tell you,
that these are the thoughts
that I have for you—
Action.

You been telling me all the things you want to do,
so put those words to action.
Show me all the freaky things you really want to do!
Deep down,
ain't no telling what I'm liable to do to ya …
put you in so many positions,
we can have our own Kama Sutra!
If you asking yourself,
Can he really do it like that?
I'm looking back at you
as if I can read your mind,
and my answer is yes!
You are in tune to the best!
I don't brag on myself,
but tonight …
I have something to prove to myself.
Come on over to my place
so we won't have any interruptions,
and I can look you in the face
when I tell you what I'm about to say.
Matter of fact, forget the talking …
let's get straight to the foreplay.
I'm looking you up and down
while your clothes hit the floor,
picking you up while we're kissing,
taking you to the bed—
there's no need to close the door!
Put you in the middle of the bed
while you speaking to me—

honestly,
I haven't paid attention to a word you've said,
because you are so sexy to me.
Kissing you deeply,
I'm loving the taste
and working my way down,
I can hardly wait.
I'm past your waist.
You moaning gently,
'cause my tongue
is in the right place,
Ooooh, Daddy!
you moan out.
I respond with a *hmmmm?*
You look down
and tell me you forgot
what you were about to say.
Don't say nothing,
just enjoy my tongue,
because I'm going all out
and I want you to remember this night from now on.
Lay you on your stomach,
lick you from the back
till you are about to cum,
whisper in your ear,
When you ready to cum,
roll me over and ride my tongue!
Now after you do that,
lay back down on your stomach …
close your legs
while I'm hitting it from the back!
You looking crazy in the face,
like you don't know what's about to happen.
You talked a good game,
now it's time for the lights, camera, and action!
Record our episode,
so when you alone
you can watch our own private show!
Watch me pick you up,
hit it fast …
turn you out,

and grind you slow …
What do you think of that?
Is that what you want, baby?
Yes, Daddy!
I want to see me getting tapped!
I told you messing around with me, that I would make you eat these words
because now you calling me
wanting second and thirds!
I told you I wasn't all about that talk,
I was all about the action,
so this situation is your fault …
this is what you get for all the lip smacking!

Happy Birthday

I couldn't shower you with kisses and gifts,
but I wanted you to know
that since I've laid eyes on you,
I've loved you so!
Beautiful to me,
gorgeous inside and out,
left me with no doubts,
of why I feel the way that I do
for you!
Today is more than just a special day,
it's your birthday,
a celebration for your years on this earth,
and to appreciate everything that
you are worth,
Let me be first,
to say,
happy birthday!
My other half
and new lifetime friend,
my partner forever,
from now until the end
of where the end takes us!
Just know that I'll always support you,
because we're a team,
and things are bigger than us
and what we are trying to do!
I love you, baby.
Just wanted to say
that though I couldn't see you face to face,
I wanted to do something special for you
on your birthday!
Here's a hug to you,
followed by a kiss!
I love you, baby,
so remember this—
we are each other's world,
but today is about you,
my favorite birthday girl!

How Can I Say

How can I say I miss you?
and give it the appropriate meaning?
How can I tell you I miss your smile
or just listening to you breathing?
My best friend
for all the right reasons—
for helping me turn dreams
into reality.
There's no need for me to keep dreaming;
all that I need
I know I have in you!
Whether right or wrong,
good times and bad,
just some things we have to go through!
I love you!
Yes!
But you know it is true,
I just don't quite understand,
why we do the things we do.
I've thought about you every day,
Wanted to hear your voice every day.
I guess we both are so stubborn
that no one wants to give way,
so instead of saying something,
or speaking up,
we let each other slip away
from each other's hands,
each other's grasp.
I still think about things we do,
smile,
and laugh!
How can I say I miss you
without you saying to yourself,
Yeah, right!
I still love you,
I just don't want to argue,
fuss or fight
with you anymore,
because arguing and these emotions

just aren't me,
and though we haven't spoken,
and I know in my heart
you have strayed away from me,
just wanted to tell you
how I feel,
because missing you
has been hard on me!
This distance is the worst.
Of course
we knew what we were doing,
just that our dreams and goals,
are in full cycle,
so our dreams and goals
are what we are pursuing.
How can I say I miss you?
I miss those beautiful eyes,
those lips;
I want to kiss you.
Guess I just told you,
in so many words,
I love you and miss you,
despite you getting on my nerves!

Thoughts to Andrea

My favorite beige chick, my favorite beige girl …
you came into my life and changed my world.
We have an unusual relationship but that is for us to figure out.
A lot of time we argue, scream, and shout;
that's our crazy way to get out our frustrations
'cause when we are face to face, it's beautiful love-making!
Now, some don't believe in love and some do
believe in love at first sight.
I don't believe in it myself, but
I was a believer that night
when we first met,
because there was a lasting impression, one I couldn't forget.
Your beautiful smile for some reason had me smiling.
I was trying to keep my cool but to myself I was lying.
Somehow I was scared to let you in
my deepest, most inner thoughts, feelings, emotions …
so I tried to pretend that I didn't care as much as I did …
But you saw right through that, 'cause near you I was acting like a lil kid.
I was scared back then, but I'm not scared now.
some way and somehow to tell you that I truly love you!
For you and what I know you would bring to the table
and whatever we can't do together, I'm willing and able
to go that extra mile and to go that extra hump
for you to realize you're all I need and all I want!
My favorite beige girl, though you make me sick,
I love you always, my favorite beige chick!
I love your smile; I love your pretty face—
Actually …
Stop …
Hold up wait …
Though we go through the things we go through,
you're always gonna be my heart and I'm always gonna love you!
Whether it's today or whether its tomorrow,
whether there is pain, doubt, and sorrow,
it's just a chance that you will have to take,
like you did from the start—I may not be able to give you what you want,
but I can take care of your heart!
Since you have been in my life, well, since you have been in my world,
it's you I've loved, my favorite beige girl!

Thoughts to Kisha

Having you in my life
has gotten me on the right path.
We share each other's company;
you constantly make me laugh.
At last I can talk to someone,
who can relate to how I feel,
not look all crazy when I express how I feel.
Is this for real?
Our conversations are cool,
even appealing.
I know how I feel,
so I can't hide my feelings.
You keep my thought open, my imaginative
process vivid.
I love you for you, from your uniqueness
to your spirit.
So thank you for being you
'cause everything you said, you
have clearly shown me and meant it.
We don't have to worry about
broken hearts, 'cause with each other
they are mended.
I've known you damn near
my whole life and never thought
this would be …
us?
Together?
You and me?
How could this be?
I laugh so hard 'cause
I know your family tree!
But I thank God, 'cause
he knew it was meant to be!
Thank you, pretty lady,
for opening my eyes up to a
whole new world, 'cause
you're in my life forever,
so here's to my favorite new girl!

Thoughts to Ms. Gilda

I loved you as much as I loved your daughter.
I was so for real when I called you
my other momma!
There were some questions
I needed to answer,
'cause the way I was feeling,
things didn't add up.
I was getting all the love
I really needed, but not from
the ones I wanted.
It was like total resentment,
heartache plus disappointment.
I always looked up to you;
whether you knew it,
I still came around, even
when I blew all of my chances.
You were looking out for your child.
I didn't understand it then, but
I truly realize now;
there aren't excuses. All I
had to do is communicate.
Maybe then we would
be in better shape.
I'm sorry I hurt
your child.
I'm sorry hurt you too!
I know that you hate me,
you dislike me and can't stand me,
but I still will always love you;
and for you, there's nothing in this world
I wouldn't do.
I try each day to be better,
so I'm finally clearing the air
starting with this letter.
I hurt not just your child
but you as well as us!
I apologize
for all the lies,
any disrespect,

all of the times
there were any cries,
shed tears,
constant fears
of me showing signs of never being there.
I hope you forgive me
for everything I did wrong,
because I am genuinely sorry,
for all of the harm.

Thoughts of Rae Sherri

I still remember the first night we stayed together.
I looked at you all night while I held you and thought,
Though we are young, I pray we grow old together.
I knew in my heart that no matter what, I
would love you always and forever!
See, our first date wasn't some fancy restaurant.
It was actually at McDonald's. I remember 'cause you
worked at the movies and I had to wait for you to get off.
We talked and talked, while gazing into each other's eyes,
while you had me bite off the tip of your fries.
I remember singing to you ...
the first time I said I love you ...
It wasn't that I was trying to spit game,
you allowed me to be me ...
which makes our love unique!
'cause there are still times when I think of you
and I feel complete.
Then there are those bad times—actually horrible times!—
when I was getting caught up with chicks and petty lies,
and though to this day I'm still sorry and I apologize,
I know it can't take back the pain and all those cries.
My love for you will never fade
nor go away!
It will always be strong and never stray!
If the opportunity presents itself where it can be,
I know I can show you I'm that man who was meant to be!
So I'll keep my prayers consistent and look up above.
Though I can't shower you with gifts,
I can give you all the love
that's needed
or meant to be
'cause that's how I feel when I think of Rae Sherri!

Being You
(Thoughts of Takeysha)

You're my everything, and I love you so much.
My heart and I appreciate everything you do.
You're so down to earth and laid back,
that's why I don't mind chilling with you.
You don't keep up no drama and your attitude
is always cool,
even when situations present themselves
for you to act a fool.
You have my back whether I'm right or wrong,
and you truly love me for me,
and don't drag me along
through any situations.
If a problem occurs,
you give your insight and observations.
Now, all of our days aren't always good;
there are times when they are bad,
and you do piss me off and
get me extremely mad.
But it doesn't mean that I don't love you!
It's just part of the process of us learning
each other; so it's some things that we have to
grow through.
I don't feel like I'm the best looking,
but you say that I'm the best
looking for you.
You make me feel comfortable
in ways others couldn't do.
It's something unique and different,
and I see it in you, but at the
same time, that's what makes me
want to be with you.
Ever since we have been together,
it's like a dream come true!
Thank you, baby, for accepting my
faults to my views,
so in other words, baby, I just
wanted to say I love you.

To My Friend Who's Dead but Never Gone

Damn, dawg, I miss you!
Though I keep quiet,
I try to do things
to uplift you.
I wear #2 to represent you.
Even though you're gone,
I still admire you.
I still take the blame,
feel ashamed
that I'm the one
who left you slain.

I should have let you come with me
and let whatever happens, happen;
and let it be.
I chose another path;
I'm sorry we clashed.
I didn't mean what I said.
Understand I was just mad.
The decision I made
I thought was right,
but it cost me in the long run,
'cause you lost your life!

My best friend
when times were good,
and when things were rough,
you had my back always,
no matter what.
I'm sorry it went down like this.
I know you can hear me,
so know that you are always missed.
I pray that you send me a sign,
just so I know that I'm heard …
so I won't feel like I'm just
mumbling words!

I hope you continue
to look down on me,
'cause I still look up to heaven.
Know that I'm doing
you proudly!
So to my best friend,
I will end it like this:
know that I
will always continue
to hold you down,
and forever you will
be missed!!

Admittance

I'm not perfect and far from the best ...
I try to be different and separate myself from the rest,
but at times I come up short.
I don't always make the best decisions,
so I believe you strip me down to see all the different dimensions.
To those that I hurt, I apologize
for the tears, the pain, and all of the cries.
For those I upset, I say that I'm sorry
for causing deceit, the disrespect, and the worries.

They say it takes a real person to admit when he is wrong,
so I will take my place and say that I was wrong.
I was wrong for a lot of things and the way I handled them,
so I'm sorry to those I hurt; I did some wrong things,
and I'll be the first to admit it.

I'm not perfect and far from the best ...
I know that life is a crazy game and I'm up for the test.
Losing your all is to rebuild and test your strength,
stop you from doing what you're doing, settle down and think.
Make wiser choices and appreciate the ones you love,
not take things for granted, be a man, and really grow up.
So I speak my piece, for my faults and wrongdoings, I confess.
I'm not perfect—far from it, but with time I do my best
to better all situations, from the good to the bad
to being a better person, individual, and dad!

I Am

I am me! Unique and creative …
I am me, a child of God …
I am …
I am the son of Melba and Hayward,
I am the brother of Elliot, Chris, and Ricky,
I am the father of Elysha …
I am not perfect,
and whether I am right or wrong,
I am me!
I am Etrec White.

Emotions ... Just Writings (EJW)

My emotions I pour out;
I let my heart bleed
through this pen.
Staining the paper with
permanent markings from
my soul from within.
Justified writings?
Naw, just writings
from my mind, which I
set free,
letting go of my imprisoned
thoughts that ramble
inside of me.
My tears sometimes smear
the flowing of my ink,
that I engrave through
these blue lined bars.
At times I smudge
my message because of
my sweaty palms.
Emotions? Yes!
Just writings? Of course.
I go to the deepest place in my heart
and let nature take its course.
I write it,
not because I can,
but because I want to
express my artistic views
the way no one thought I could do.
So dark clouds will never
cloud me;
I will continue to keep shining.
Forever my emotions will be
just writings!

SEXUAL HEALING:
Erotic Pleasures

Feeling Freaky

Take off everything; baby, lay down.
I don't care about your weight and I don't care about your size;
tonight we making love, so hold me tight and close your eyes.
I'm feeling freaky, so sit up and open your legs,
'cause I want to taste your sweet spot
while I'm giving you this head!
Grab my head and position me how you want me to lick it.
After you nut on my tongue, I can slide in and stick it!
I feel your tightness, and your moans are turning me on, and I feel you cummin',
'cause it's creamy and warm. I'm going deeper and harder; and you telling me you
love me! I'm constantly stroking it, while you saying, *Etrec ... ooooh! Fuck me!*
You're so wet that now I'm slippin' out, so let me get it from the back; close your
legs while you moan and shout! Get in the mood, no need to be sneaky. I had to
send you this 'cause at this moment, I was feeling freaky!

All the Different Ways

There's so many different ways I love to get your pussy wet—
meeting you in the shower and kissing them lips and sucking on that neck,
laying you down and just sucking on your pussy I know will get you wet,
or you on your stomach, pushing yourself up with your legs open
while I lick you from the back—the position I love best!

Matter of fact, let me get some ice and explore that pussy right now.
Getting you real wet, having you slippery and gushy.
You used to me being soft and mushy, but, tonight it's all about
you and my pretty wet pussy!

Fuck it, clear everything off the table, for a night you won't forget …
'cause for me, you my dinner and all I want is some
honey, strawberry syrup, and my tongue on your clit!

I wanna lick you up, baby, and I wanna lick you down,
I wanna make you scream and shout, so tonight is something different—
it's all about your pussy in my mouth; it's without a doubt
I'm feeling freaky, so hold me tight—
naw, baby just squeeze me!

Don't let me go; tell me that you need me!

Let me lay on my back so I can feel you ride my tongue,
and I can hold onto your ass and feel you let loose
when I feel you cum!

Can I stand you up and have your pressed up against the door
while I kiss you on the back of your neck and I'm fingering you,
so I can feel you bust on my finger, saying, *Daddy, give me more*?

There's so many different ways I love to feel you get wet,
but all these ways are the ways I love best!

Hitting Your Spot

I can tell I'm hitting your spot
from the way your body shakes.
You shaking the bed, which is shaking the room
like we having an earthquake.
Baby, hold on! Stop! Don't move!
Ahhh, shit! Wait!
I'm not hearing none of that,
so it's not up for debate!
Shhh, lay back down and go back to sleep;
You will get another round as soon as you wake.

I can tell that I'm hitting your spot,
You biting down on the pillow telling me to stop
'cause your juices are flowing nonstop!
You dripping so hard with your beads of sweat
I can feel every drop.
While you're on the bottom, I'm on top
giving you all the sexual healing you need
while I'm getting my point across.
Keep reaching and moaning and calling me your boss,
'cause these are all the things you do while I'm hitting your spot!

Frisky Feelings

So, you going to keep looking at me,
looking sexy as shit?
You already turned on 'cause
you keep biting your bottom lip.
This whole time it's been nothing
but playful seduction,
and between your legs is
a watery eruption!
Your clit is jumping,
more like your pussy is thumping …
all of these feelings, and
I ain't really said nothing.
You saying no but your body
is definitely saying yes.
You constantly kissing me,
putting me to the test!
Now you thinking will I leap
to your bait,
'cause you want me so bad,
you can hardly wait
to feel my touch
all over your body
'cause you feeling freaky and
ready to get naughty.
You looking out the window;
in the yard, you see the lawn chair.
Maan, come do me right now, so
I can put this ass in the air,
and whoever sees us, it's whatever,
'cause I really don't care!
You tell me all of this willingly,
and taking you up on this offer
is all too easy but
I can't right now, plus,
this ain't the time, nor the place.
I'd rather have you somewhere
romantic, where I can make love
to you and see your pretty face,
or watch you get out of the shower,

dry off, and put that outfit on with the lace.
Hold on and wait for that moment;
I promise you won't be disappointed!
I'm sorry, baby, but please understand
that I want you to melt all over me,
not just in my hand!

Late Night Special

The lights are dim, and you looking so sexy
I can't wait to feel your body next to me,
with those soft-ass lips, you kissing me softly,
my mind is all over the place, thinking erotically.
You riding me hard, while I'm looking at you biting your bottom lip
with that, *Damn, this dick!*
look in your eyes.
I'm mesmerized and feeling so gone
'cause we making love all night long.
Now I'm on top of you with your legs crossed as they
are on my shoulder and I'm stroking you deep,
and you whisper in my ear, *This the type*
of shit that will put me to sleep!
It's nothing, baby; I'll do this J. Holiday style.
Let me put you to bed, but before that, let me eat you for a while!
I got some ice in my mouth;
let me run it across your clit, mixing the ice with
A lil cool water, your nut, and my spit!
Now it's my turn, and you got my eyes to roll
while you flexing your pussy all over my pole!
Doing shit like that is gonna make me spoiled
'cause I keep nuttin', and its outta control.
I'm loving it, baby, 'cause you got me feeling freaky,
and we done used up all the syrup and we sticky,
you telling me, *Daddy, bust this nut and fall asleep in me!*
I really want to, but it ain't that easy!
Well, okay … here goes nothing …
I got it out, and I look you in the eyes
as we both look at each other to a beautiful sunrise.
You tell me to go to sleep, 'cause this was a whole other level,
as you whisper in my ear, *Thank you for the late night special.*

ABOUT THE AUTHOR

Etrec White was born on February 5, 1978, to Melba Dale and Hayward White. Etrec was raised in Jacksonville, Florida, and spent most of his youth playing sports, which included football, basketball, martial arts, and baseball. He played most of these sports during his school years and for local community teams. It was also during this time that he found he had a real passion and talent for writing. Whenever he felt down or unable to express himself, Etrec took to the pen and wrote down his feelings.

This outlet has continued to work for him during every aspect of his life. Whether it was school, relationships, family, or friends that were on his mind, he wrote until he couldn't write any more. These are the writings that allowed him to create *Emotions … Just Writings (EJW)*.